INCREDIBLE EDIBLE

SEEDS TO SOLUTIONS

THE POWER OF SMALL ACTIONS

PAM WARHURST CBE

ANNE SIKKING

First published
November 2021
by

INCREDIBLE EDIBLE CIC

© Incredible Edible CIC
www.incredibleedible.org.uk

© Jonathon Porritt 2021 – FOREWORD

Book design:
Bob Jackson

Typeset in:
Montserrat and Londrina Solid

Printed in:
Italy by SPADA Media

Paper:
Sourced from sustainable forests

Compiled and produced for INCREDIBLE EDIBLE CIC
by
SP SQUARE CIC
Scotland
www.spsquare.org

ISBN 978-1-5272994-6-7

TABLE OF CONTENTS

PART ONE - IN THE BEGINNING

PART TWO - PROOF OF CONCEPT

PART THREE - POINTING A WAY

PART FOUR - NEXT STEPS

PART FIVE

PART ONE

IN THE BEGINNING

FOREWORD – JONATHON PORRITT

Let's face it: this is one hell of a difficult time to stay cheerful about things. The drum-beat of doom provides a constant backdrop to our lives: accelerating climate change: COVID-19; economic pressures and worsening inequality; species at risk; habitats and special places heedlessly destroyed; local services stretched thinner and thinner – it just goes on and on.

I've lived with that for decades, even as the drum-beat has got louder and louder. The only way I've kept going is constantly to seek out a very different musical backdrop: upbeat, joyful, irreverent, loving, and charged with the kind of positive energy that not just makes it possible to keep on keeping on, but to celebrate at least as much as to mourn, to be uplifted at least as often as to be downcast.

So what's the trick? Throw in your lot with people and organisations working in service to others, doing stuff rather than theorising about it, making things better for people, communities and future generations, obstinately and creatively working the angles to deliver lasting solutions – often against unbelievable odds.

Which I guess is where Incredible Edible came into my life, more or less 20 years ago, when the indomitable Pam Warhurst pointedly suggested to the Sustainable Development Commission (of which I was then Chair) that we should be focused at least as much on local things as on national policy (and much less on Whitehall in particular!), and that Incredible Edible Todmorden was as good a place to start out on that journey as anywhere else in the UK. And so it proved to be!

I've stayed in touch with Pam and Incredible Edible since then, and have been vaguely aware of how that particular Todmorden seed has been growing and growing. But until I was asked to write the Foreword to Seeds to Solutions (which meant reading every one of the wondrous 'case studies' you're about to be regaled with!), I had no idea of just how much it had grown.

I defy anyone not to be both inspired and deeply moved by Seeds to Solutions. The diversity of places where the Incredible Edible seeds have been planted is in itself a revolution – from the usual streets, squares and green spaces through to schools, hospitals, housing estates, residential homes and all sorts of wasteland crying out for some deep green repurposing.

It's also been so instructive to learn from the Tips of all those who've done the hard graft, and to have my culinary imagination so enticingly stimulated by all the Recipes. I can't wait to have a crack at Elderflower Fritters (see page 53) when our hedgerows go crazy with all those abundant blooms all over again in May next year!

But my abiding takeaway from Seeds to Solutions are the stories of the multitude of individuals involved in these amazing case studies – the extent of whose endeavour is often only hinted at, with readers left to fill in the gaps, to feel our way into the struggles, the ups and downs, the crazy emotional rollercoasters that peek out between the lines.

So I end with my personal thanks to all of those Incredible Edible volunteers for their ongoing dedication and joyful inspiration.

September 2021

PAM WARHURST

BACK IN THE DAY

There comes a time in everyone's life when it's put up or shut up.

That time for me was in 2008 when Professor Tim Lang spoke at a conference on the implications of climate change and food supply – how overuse of the world's resources by the rich and comfortable had paved the way for climatic pressures that would bring misery to millions and hit the poorest the most.

None of this was news to me really. As I sat on the train back to Manchester my mind went back to 1992. I reflected on my naive excitement as a council leader to see 172 nations coming together under the banner of the United Nations Conference on Environment and Development, known as the Rio de Janeiro Earth Summit, to square up to the impending threat of climate change. An unprecedented meeting of representatives from across the globe, all focused on the changes needed to rein in those human activities that were taking their toll on our planet and the scientific knowledge that underpinned what those changes might look like.

World leaders devised plans and wrote draft policies. Their advisors devised rallying cries like "Think Global, Act local". Academics made careers out of the publications they put their names to. And yet, other than the amazing dedication at a local government level to deliver what became known as Local Agenda 21, where in the years to come were the brave big ticket incentives we needed particularly in Western economies? Where was the encouragement at pace to move to more sustainable lifestyles?

Other Earth Summits came and went and after each one was an increasing sense that these elected leaders really couldn't smell the coffee of the global warming catastrophes that were only just over their time horizons.

Chair of Incredible Edible CIC.

Pam is the co-founder of Incredible Edible Todmorden and founder of the movement worldwide. Her life long work in food, health, and the environment extends from early work in wholefood collectives through to being Leader of Calderdale Council, chair of an NHS trust, Deputy Chair of The Countryside Agency, and Chair of the Forestry Commission. Her TED talk on Incredible Edible, and her global work to connect grassroots food growing to communities, learning, and enterprise is internationally acknowledged.

"WE HAVE IT IN US, ALL OF US, TO BE MAGNIFICENT IN A CRISIS, AND MY, WE ARE IN A CRISIS.

In fairness the UK Government in 2008 introduced The Climate Change Act which made the UK the first country in the world to establish a long term legally binding framework to cut carbon emissions – net zero by 2050.

But frameworks are not boots on the ground. The science was screaming at us to change and change now. We needed more than hope, we needed action.

Recent history had demonstrated that procrastination ruled OK at a government level, that the economy trumped all other games in town, and that technology would save the day. I begged to differ. Nothing I'd seen since Rio gave me any confidence that this approach could be trusted to deliver the change needed in the time available, which was getting shorter by the month. My child's future mattered. The future of children I'd never meet mattered. And I was damned if I wasn't going to do whatever I could, however small, to fight for that better future.

So on that train back to Manchester a thought popped into my head that still leaves the hairs on the back of my neck standing. We the people could lead the way. We could stop being done to and start doing. We could stop waiting for those leaders to be brave, and get on creating that kinder future for ourselves. We could demonstrate the changes needed in the places we called home, and use that experience to bring about change at a national level. Ambitious, but what's to lose!

To me the logic was compelling. We needed a different approach. Some breakthrough management from the grassroots up. We hadn't got time to dither. They'd done it down the road from me in Rochdale nearly two hundred years before when a bunch of folks started buying food collectively and sharing it with others at prices folks could afford. From that visionary act of survival came the world wide Cooperative Movement.

We have it in us, all of us, to be magnificent in a crisis, and my, we are in a crisis. But hairs on the back of a neck are one thing. Finding the way into this positive rethink of people and planet, that's something else. And it all had to be done by avoiding the usual channels: by cutting the chains of 'business as usual'; by acting quickly to demonstrate what change looks like; by exploding myths around the need for a bureaucracy and turning the negatives of deprivation into a celebration of aspiration.

These thoughts were the fuel that drove me to a blindingly obvious conclusion. What is the common thread that brings us together across age, income culture and ability? What is it that we can get our teeth into without professional qualifications, permissions or big budgets controlled by external funders?

The answer of course is food.

So activities around local food would be the Trojan Horse that took us, simply by the way we lived our lives, into a different relationship with each other and the planet.

It was all an experiment. It had to be kicked off by volunteers.

And it needed a simple model that we could all get involved with, that we could interpret according to circumstances but that defined us as being Incredible Edible. The idea of three spinning plates seemed to fit the bill.

Community was one plate – growing food to share in very public propaganda gardens. Searching out the skills we need to grow and cook from within the community was the Learning plate. Supporting local growers and producers through our weekly spend led us to the Business plate. Together they make a sticky money economy. No government directive needed. All a reflection of everyday life if local food was at the heart of our new normal.

And here's the aside on that. We were not going to be cute little community activists who could be patted on the back for best endeavours, or fobbed off with being cited as a best practice case study. Believe me, if you really don't want to change a system, you celebrate best practice and then move on to the next thing on the list of how to maintain status quo. But more of that

> **VILLAGE OR BOROUGH, ISLAND OR ESTATE, IT'S THE PEOPLE THAT DEFINE THEMSELVES AS INCREDIBLE EDIBLE NOT THE POLICY MAKERS OR PROFESSIONALS.**

later...

So I got off the train, in Todmorden, went straight to the best community activist and networker I know, my friend Mary Clear and, together with a small bunch of locals, Incredible Edible the experiment went from concept to reality in next to no time. It didn't start life with that name by the way. That was Mary's daughter, whose answer to, 'What shall we call it that says everything we want in a couple of words', was 'Incredible Edible'. Perfect.

Those early days were so exciting. We knew we were onto something. The reaction we'd got from a meeting we'd advertised in a cafe was electric. The buzz was tangible. Folks were ready for change. More local food growing, more people learning the how's and what's of local food, more jobs, the creation of a sticky money economy, simply through people's purchase of what was produced locally. None of it was original. None of it was rocket science. It was just joined up thinking about the way we all live our lives but with a more local focus.

We walked down streets that could be filled with food. These became our propaganda gardens. We could learn how to grow and cook it by others in our community showing us how. In other words this was reconnecting community and the lost arts. We could spend more of our money on local not international, creating our sticky money economy where the profit stays where the spend is. Sustainable development results without any grandiose fanfare.

The stories in this book are testament to the amazing strength, imagination and compassion of thousands of Incredibles who just get on and do it, not talk about it. Village or borough, island or estate, it's the people that define themselves as Incredible Edible not the policy makers or professionals. The power and passion the groups release is contagious. We are all part of a local food movement whose influence is felt in sectors way beyond the food sector itself. Collectively all Incredible Edibles have experiences to offer up to anyone who takes the time to explore why we do what they do and what we have learned in the doing. And, as Mary would say, that's where

"INVESTMENTS, WHETHER LOTTERY OR TREASURY, NEED TO BE MEASURED BY THEIR TOTAL IMPACT ON SOCIETY, SPECIES AND PLANET, NOT SIMPLY THE OUTDATED METRIC OF FISCAL PRUDENCE.

the other hand clapping comes in.

All this activity, personal investment, and sheer grit of the citizen needs to be matched by the release of the brave and insightful in our major institutions to become the servant leaders of the future. Policy frameworks from planning to well-being, from regeneration to education, need to change to become the wind under the wings of the grassroots activists, not the means to clip those wings. New contracts need to be drawn up between citizen and state to allow all to play to their strengths and collectively prepare society for the unpredictable impacts of a changing climate.

Investments, whether lottery or treasury, need to be measured by their total impact on society, species and planet, not simply the outdated metric of fiscal prudence. None of us went to university to discover this. We just signed up to be Incredible. As many have said. 'If you eat you're in.'

We've lived the impact of generosity and kindness. We've met people and learned tricks we never knew existed. We've come to respect the awesomeness of nature from a tiny seed becoming a delicious meal to a reconnection with the seasons, seeing time as our friend not our enemy.

So, from all these thirteen years of learning, what's on my priority list for the systems change that we must all have the confidence to embrace and invest in?

Well health's a no brainier. We need a much healthier population if we're to keep people out of the doctors and help our medics prepare for the next major health crisis that sadly will come our way. More than ten years ago in Todmorden we started to build the bridge between our NHS local health centre and healthy lifestyles by taking up the prickly inedible plants that had been landscaped around it and growing fruit trees and bushes, herbs and vegetables. To us it just seemed like a better idea than running multi-million pound campaigns about "Eat five a day", whilst still having patients walk to their clinic through uninspiring inedibles to get their

"REPURPOSE THE PUBLIC REALM, LET PEOPLE GROW FOR THEIR COMMUNITY ON IT, AND IT IS THEN THAT YOU START TO MAKE INROADS FROM THE GRASSROOTS UP. A COMMUNITY RIGHT TO GROW. WHY NOT!

prescription, (and there wasn't social prescribing at the time).

This simple activity is now replicated all over the place as Incredible Edible groups demonstrate putting health back into the NHS. But the question is, how might the logic behind the actions become mainstream? The first of our systems change asks of the NHS is to:

· Make edible landscaping mainstream with community enterprises contracted to maintain them.
· Invest in community kitchens to capitalise on this increased interest in locally grown food, bringing medic, patient and community together and upskilling many to prepare great meals for their family and neighbourhood from nutritious ingredients grown right under their noses.
· Bend your considerable budgets in support of local enterprises rather than huge conglomerates giving a signal to the market that local supply chains are here to stay and should be widely supported.
· Use metrics of success that go beyond the fiscal and with the huge reach and public support for our health services influence others to follow your lead.

Where next? Well it's about time we had a long look at that misnamed public realm. The success of our groups so often depends on a local authority, housing association or other public body saying 'yes' when asked if locals can grow food to share.

Many do say 'yes'. Some don't. Some say 'yes', but eventually default to 'no'. And yet access to good food, and a knowledge of what to do with it, has to be the foundation of a healthier society. Issues of food justice, sovereignty, fair share, are on the agendas of every Local Authority. Reduced food miles, air quality, carbon reductions and sequestration are top of the list for many government departments. Throw in community cohesion, reinvention of the High Street, new planning laws and you're starting to list the pressure public bodies are faced with against ever decreasing budgets.

"WE THE PEOPLE COULD LEAD THE WAY. WE COULD STOP BEING DONE TO AND START DOING. WE COULD STOP WAITING FOR THOSE LEADERS TO BE BRAVE, AND GET ON CREATING THAT KINDER FUTURE FOR OURSELVES.

start to make inroads from the grassroots up. A community right to grow. Why not!

All of the above, and so much more, is what we've learned together across the years. We started as an experiment, which in truth we still are, but what a magnificent experiment – of its time – powered by people and a simple truth which shone like a beacon from the soil at the heart of our communities. Believe in the power of small actions. Together we can change the rules and with that our future.

...SCIENCE WAS SCREAMING AT US TO CHANGE AND CHANGE NOW. WE NEEDED MORE THAN HOPE, WE NEEDED ACTION.

PART TWO

PROOF OF CONCEPT

ANNE SIKKING

STORIES FROM THE GRASSROOTS

We didn't want a beige book. This is just as well, since we didn't get one. There is no even style in Seeds to Solutions. There are barely any formatting rules in terms of punctuation and layout. Instead – like Berkley University, reportedly installing the walkways a year after it opened, by laying paving where people had left their tracks – we adjusted to the contributors. The design was stretched to fit the words and pictures we were sent, the quality of which varies. The text was laid in, more or less true to the expression of the people themselves. As for the recipes, some tempted us, so we made them ourselves and enjoyed them. However, like the rest of the text they are not written in a standard format. Most have been tested only by those who submitted them. (Cooks beware!) The voice oscillates between first person accounts, and those written as we, or they, he or she. We hope their many individual and colourful personalities ring out.

In terms of content, for some, the focus is on the beans and herbs, for others, it's on people finding their way from custodial care back to mainstream society, or eating more healthily, or enjoying the outdoors, or teaching their children, or battling stress, or creating art and music, or all them. There are bee-lines, orchards, dog poo clearances, performances, market stalls, cooking sessions, railways, jams, cakes, foragers, works of art, food banks, pantries, even song lyrics, to name but some. There is compost and digging – lots of compost and digging - and used pallets of course. The groups are all ages, all abilities, all shapes, sizes, cultures. And these groups represent only a small percentage of groups operating worldwide.

Some groups began with 'ordinary' people around a kitchen table. Just as Pam Warhurst and Mary Clear who, in 2007, bent over mugs of coffee wanting an answer the question, 'what can we do?' These two individuals then went on to create the international phenomena that is Incredible

Co-author of Seeds to Solutions and board member of Incredible Edible CIC.

Writer. Parent. Cook. Novelist. Poet. A lifetime of working in and promoting social enterprise has allowed Anne to develop food enterprises with marginalised people – women, people transitioning from custodial care, entrepreneurs of both Afro-Caribbean and Asian heritage – some of whom are still trading. The same skills took her into proposing, implementing and managing transnational projects for the EU, and then on into founding and running plant-based restaurants for more than two decades. In 2020 she was appointed Poet Laureate for an arts magazine in the south bay area of Los Angeles. She now works with SP SQUARE, reverse action publishers, whose speciality is using new ways to publish ideas too often overlooked.

"IT'S AS IF INCREDIBLE EDIBLE PROVIDED EVERYONE WITH THE SAME SET OF COAT HOOKS, BUT, ON VISITING EACH HOUSEHOLD, WE FIND THAT THE THINGS HANGING FROM THE HOOKS DIFFER.

Edible. Not just about community gardens, or even guerilla gardening, that first Incredible Edible began planting up food in public spaces, drawing in local people from all backgrounds, engaging high profile service providers such as the police and fire stations, working with schools to expand the curriculum and to change the dinner menus, to key into hydroponics. That first Incredible Edible encouraged local businesses to benefit from their capacity to both source and sell local food production. *Incredible! Plant Veg, Grow a Revolution* by Pam Warhurst and Joanne Dobson (isbn 978-1-78306-487-8) charts this remarkable journey from back-water market town in the north of England to a global exemplar of transformation.

Similarly, some of today's Incredible Edible activity has been implemented by public officials wishing to improve things in their locality. They have seen that the ethos of Incredible Edible works, as a means to strengthen communities. They have noticed the mental and physical health benefits that stem from locally produced food. They are aware of the economic benefits of 'vegetable tourism'. Some are supporting big ideas about getting more local food production into local eateries by setting up central locations for cleaning and preparing vegetables so that the end user can receive it in a state fit for their use. Everywhere there is more and more awareness of the need for a more circular, more inclusive, economy. Increasingly we hear words like 'resilience' and 'kindness' being spoken aloud by public sector staff and included in strategy documents. When it comes to town planning, to food, to the health and wealth of communities, there is a new vernacular emerging.

Given all of this variety, it's unsurprising that no two contributions in Seeds to Solutions are the same. Yet all share an ethos of working together, about adapting to circumstances, about creating community, about learning and teaching new things, about enterprise in its most basic form. It's as if Incredible Edible provided everyone with the same set of coat hooks, but, on visiting each household, we find that the things hanging from the hooks differ from home to home. In this variety of contributions the very ethos of Incredible Edible is at work, not just in the diverse contents of the book but also in its compilation – a blessed chaos of experiences, yet all with a family resemblance.

During the six months it took to pull this book together I have communicated with literally hundreds of people. At last count the emails alone are numbered in the thousands. As the pages of Seeds to Solutions show, they have all enthused about their groups. At times they have also despaired, about things like the weather, access to land, too little money, not enough time, pests, the slow speed of change. But none has ever said it wasn't worth it. Even the group who was forced to stop, whose hard work was torn up, have had the grace to see that operating made a difference. The very people who forced them to stop are now, for the first time, planting an edible landscape.

I wonder if, when seeing Seeds to Solutions in print, the people in these Incredible Edible groups will be surprised to find that they are fêted by those who sit in the House of Lords, that their example is influencing lawmakers, that their achievements are being saluted by university professors, that they are attracting reverence from activists and policy makers alike. I wonder if they will marvel at how all the wet feet, false starts, aching backs, have taken us to a very different place, where, because of their fortitude and endurance, Incredible Edible members are being listened to by churches, by government, by global corporations. There is a shift happening.

So it may be also be a surprise for the groups who contributed to this book to see themselves in a book, not just alongside a huge corporation like COMPASS plc, but to see that the ethos of their grassroots actions is now being adopted and developed by that huge company as a transferable model for other similarly large organisations. When one is deep in something it's easy to miss the bigger picture. This bigger picture is what Pam Warhurst, as the Chair of Incredible Edible CIC, and we, as board members under her guidance, hold on to and are now using to take the work reported here to the next level. At the same time, this book, like Incredible Edible itself, is a growing concern, more and

"INCREDIBLE EDIBLE (WHILE OF COURSE BEING PARTLY ABOUT GROWING CABBAGES) IS FUNDAMENTALLY ABOUT GROWING CAPACITY, CAPACITY FOR CHANGE, FOR TRANSFORMATION, FOR INTERWOVEN RELATIONSHIPS.

> ## AS THE PAGES SHOW, PEOPLE HAVE ALL ENTHUSED ABOUT THEIR GROUPS. AT TIMES THEY HAVE ALSO DESPAIRED, ABOUT THINGS LIKE THE WEATHER, ACCESS TO LAND... BUT NONE HAS EVER SAID IT WASN'T WORTH IT.

more groups will add to it as the digital version is developed.

When Isaac Newton wrote his modern version of the ancients, 'we are building on the shoulders of giants', his idea was not that we see further, or have greater insight, because we are better than those who went before us, but rather that our vision is better because others before us boost us up to a better vantage point. For Incredible Edible, however, the exact the opposite may be true. Today's giants, such as a multi-national food business, are able to extend their reach, use their size to get us all where we need to be far faster than grassroots groups can, because they can stand on the shoulders of the 'ordinary' people. The Incredible Edible groups worldwide have painstakingly proven the concept – when you put food at the centre of the plan, the strategy, the life, everything is drawn in, and the resulting loops of sustainability are elastic and inclusive.

Without that moment in Todmorden with Pam and Mary, the groups recorded in this book would not be telling us their stories. Without these group stories we would not have the Incredible Edible proof of concept that is now inspiring a changes on a large scale: the law to permit public access to public land; multinational moves to hyper-localising food supplies; new understandings of how to live with climate change creatively whilst halting its continued damage.

As with Pam and Mary, just two people in a kitchen, setting in motion these groups here, now, all across the world, many more like them have done the same. By 'the same', I don't mean groups of people growing cabbages. Incredible Edible is no more about growing cabbages than a menu is a dinner. Incredible Edible (while of course being partly about growing cabbages) is fundamentally about growing capacity, capacity for change, for transformation, for interwoven human relationships. They have been a joy to work with and we owe them an incalculable debt.

ABERGELE & PENSARN
WALES

WHERE

Abergele, together with its smaller suburb Pensarn, is a sea-side community on the Irish sea, near to Conwy in north Wales. A place of immense natural beauty and, as is common in Wales, it has an abundance of castles and historical sites like the iron age fort and the Peel. The Harp Inn is believed to have been built on the site of a medieval prison & still has cells underneath. Features of St Michaels church can be dated to the 14th Century.

WHO

The five of us; Pam Luckock, Cerren Wyn Richards, Janette Gilbourne, Glenys Owen-Jones & Anna Cole, have had the welcome support and guidance of the Incredible Edible Conwy Town beacon group.

WHAT

We grow a selection of edible herbs including mint, parsley, camomile, fenugreek, chives, borage, fennel, marjoram and thyme. Vegetables, strawberries, raspberries and pollinator plants such as marigolds, nasturtiums and selection of bee friendly wildflowers are in containers around the town.

TIPS

· Find your nearest Incredible Edible group and get them to guide you.

· Don't rule out a formal structure for the group, but do evaluate how best to operate. For now we think we are best left as a loose group of committed neighbours.

· Resist pressure from others if feeling pushed to take on things you are not comfortable with.

"THERE SEEMS TO BE A GENEALOGY HERE OF WELLNESS, PLANTS, IDEAS, AND HOPE FOR THE FUTURE.

LETTUCE SOUP / CAWL LETYS

· 1 medium onion
· leaves of any lettuce- bolted leaves will do!
· a handful of peas (fresh or frozen)
· 1 vegetable stock cube
· a few mint leaves
· water to cover
pressure cook 5 mins
blend
serve hot or cold with a dollop of vegan or dairy cream.

Mwynhewch!/ Enjoy!

Many of our food ideas are inspired by Hugh Fearnley-Whittingstall.

STORIES

In response to recent correspondence about 'Seeds to Solutions' our small group wish to offer a story as a contribution to the book, straight from our hearts.

We've come to realise that our Friday morning WhatsApp chats, held every week during the lockdown/pandemic, in place of our community garden meet-ups, have kept us feeling very 'well' and have enriched our friendship. The conversations have sustained both ourselves and our belief that by taking small gentle actions we can influence local change for good. This is the inspirational ethos of Incredible Edible.

In respect of the sourcing of plants, one of our group has done a fantastic job of sourcing the herb and food plants from her garden.

Recently, with a new member in the group and a couple of musician supporters from a local ceilidh band, we added more plants from our gardens to the table and hosted our very first plant share in the walled garden at a local park.

After weeks of poor weather and months of COVID restrictions, we had chosen a glorious sunny afternoon. We set up our tables and strung the lovingly sewn Incredible Edible bunting, only made the night before! It was a small impromptu gathering, sharing plants, conversation, music, ideas and friendship.

Four new people signed up to join us almost doubling the group! An impromptu invitation to share cheese scones and a cuppa ended a perfect afternoon!

We have our fingers crossed that there may be a story for you here. A story that conveys the simple pleasures of Incredible Edible.

60%

COMMUNITY

30%

LEARNING

10%

BUSINESS

Our Incredible Edible group is currently a project of a local community group, Abergele District Action Group. We work closely with other local community groups including Youthshedz. Two of our planters are outside the library. Of course being bi-lingual may help us to connect more broadly with the community.

We work with the forest school teacher at a local school & are in touch with other local schools and youth groups. Covid interrupted plans for a project with local primary school pupils. We hope to get this started in 2022. We are learning how to support one another in encouraging young people to get involved.

We encourage local business to adopt the 'shop local' initiatives. Our local veg shop gave us free trays of plants. We have a few businesses that have supported us by allowing small Incredible Edible planters to be sited outside their premises. We plan to build on this.

ABERGELE & PENSARN

ACASSUSO
ARGENTINA

WHERE

Our garden is in a public space bordering the railroad, in the San Isidro district about 20 km from Buenos Aires city centre. The area is residential, commercial, and gastronomic with a lot of cultural and tourist activity. The street alongside of the garden is quite busy and many pedestrians walk along beside it. It is in a highly visible place.

WHO

In October 2019 Alejandra Igarzábal saw a TED talk by Pam Warhurst and from that time onwards began to wonder about how the Incredible Edible principles could be applied in her area. In some ways the project arose spontaneously, during the full Covid quarantine of July 2020 when several neighbours, Jorge, Elena, Ale china, Christian, Vilma, Olga, Rosario, Miluca, Claudia, Cami, Lucrecia, Juan José, Lily, Vale, Laura, Clarisa, Gabriela, Bea, Silvia and Juani, without all knowing each other, began to participate and collaborate in establishing the garden, most being women. Once a week they now get together and are committed to the project on a voluntary basis. Sometimes children come and activities are organised. We've also been blessed to have had the wonderful talents of Adela Guardone who has taken the photographs we are sharing here.

WHAT

We have transformed a piece of land that had rubble, garbage, dog poop, on it into a kind place, both natural, and beautiful. There are flowers, beneficial to butterflies and other insects which have begun to come and expand the biodiversity which improves the environment. Families and children come to learn where the vegetables come from and are encouraged to harvest these themselves and take them home to eat. There are garden boxes and terraces on the ground. We also set up a greenhouse tunnel for seedlings. Along with the deep beds we have also added compost bins, as a way to raise awareness among the neighbours, who bring their organic waste to recycle. This becomes the mature compost we use to fertilize the soil organically.

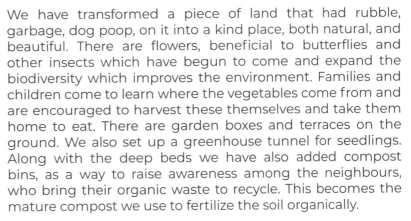

TIPS

· Consider not asking permission to start a garden.

· Try to have a nice and neat aesthetic. Hide buckets, plastic bags, plates.

· Make an anti-dog fence.

· Use used car oil (it's free), to protect any wood, and it is also a way to recycle it.

· Have a garden and compost, so that the process is as sustainable as possible.

· Ensure biodiversity in vegetables and flowers to attract beneficial insects and repel pests. Choose to cultivate native plants that attract butterflies.

· Have a fixed day and time in the week to meet in the garden.

· Do activities with children, eg planting in seedlings, setting up an insect hotel.

"LET'S CELEBRATE LIFE AND SING, THANKING THE EARTH FOR ALL IT BRINGS. LET US BE HAPPY AS WE SOW, BE HAPPY TO SHARE AS WE GO. (*TRADITIONAL*)

LAVENDER MUFFINS

· Preheat the oven to 180°C.
· Mix together 1 cup of flour with 1 tsp of baking powder, 2 tablespoons of chopped lavender leaves, 2 eggs, ¼ cup of oil, 1/3 cup of sugar and 1/3 cup of milk.
· Pour into muffin moulds and bake 12 minutes or until golden and a knife comes out clean.

STORIES

At the beginning we had raised beds, but it was difficult for us to find good soil to fill them. So when we discovered that the soil of our plot of land was quite good, we decided to make terraces using the bio-intensive methods of John Jeavons. We did the double digging; we had to use a pick, since there were stones that we could not remove with the shovel. It was amusing that when police patrol cars passed they preferred not to look at us...we were ladies digging in a public space!

Another challenge was irrigation, since there was no tap in the place, we had to go to a neighbour's, to get water. Then somebody donated a water tank to us, and now the municipality has taken the responsibility to be in charge of filling it.

Ants are a problem; We try to control them by leaving them orange peel and rice.

Another issue is the theft of vegetables. So now we have put up a blackboard where we have written that we harvest together on Wednesdays. This is to let people know that this is something shared and participatory and also for everyone.

An unforeseen challenge was the opposition of some neighbours to having a garden and compost heap in this residential neighbourhood, since they associate it with lower social classes. We have invited them to come and meet us and talk, but we still have not had an answer...

It was incredible to see how from the moment we put the first raised bed by the railway, neighbours joined in. The garbage collectors, very happy with the undertaking, even gave us gloves as gifts! We celebrate community events; birthdays, Pachamama (Mother Earth Day) and Spring. Conversations arise, new friendships between neighbours who had never spoken to each other, generate a sense of community that enriches us, respecting the land and nature in a more conscious and grateful way.

COMMUNITY

As there is little gardening culture in Buenos Aires, we had to train ourselves. We did the bio-intensive garden workshop with Fernando Pia, who has been making organic gardens in Patagonia for 35 years. It was he who told us about Pamela Warhurst and Incredible Edible. In addition to the community garden, several of us have made gardens on our sidewalks and balconies, helping us to set them up, and exchanging seeds, plants and knowledge. Sometimes we organize activities for children, where we teach them to sow in a seedbed, to transplant and to water. We try to convey what we learned to adults who ask specific questions. We organise various learning talks; eg composting, sowing methods, slurry production, etc.

LEARNING

Urban gardens in Buenas Aires in general, and in our neighbourhood in particular, started recently, and therefore the commercial aspect is still incipient. Having written that, however, our garden is a few blocks from a commercial and gastronomic centre, with which there are several possibilities to connect with an enterprise. As people, young and old, become familiar with the gardens and learn how to grow our food organically, it will motivate them to want to consume products whose preparation is as natural as possible. And so we suggest that, before long, in the vicinity of any urban garden, a circulating "Mercado de Barrio", or community wealth building, will soon be created.

BUSINESS

ACASSUSO

WHERE

In semi-rural Wales, within the grounds of a large 18th century residential home, lurks an exclusive Incredible Edible garden, not open to the general public. The grounds are dominated by ancient oaks overlooking lawns, a small pond and a vegetable garden. This garden isn't open to the general public as the participants have one thing in common: a lengthy period of incarceration. This approved premises residential facility is a place where people recently released from prison re-encounter life on the outside. Residents stay for a few weeks or a few months, and many of them participate in the Incredible Edible garden, growing food to share with others in the community.

WHO

This Incredible Edible vegetable garden attracts mainly older men who've been locked up for several years. As they begin to construct a new post-prison life, long hours are spent in the garden. They talk about the attraction of the fresh air, the smell of the soil and the fresh flavour of a vegetable plucked from the ground. Other residents, who know nothing of plants, enjoy taking up the responsibility of watering, digging up beds or the woodwork associated with raised beds. The garden attracts residents looking to while away a few hours on a sunny afternoon or who are itching to spend weeks elbows-deep in engrossing physical activity. For reasons which should be obvious, this contribution to Seeds to Solutions must remain an anonymous one.

WHAT

The vegetable garden is a mix of poly-tunnels containing raised beds as well as a number of outdoor beds. There are also a number of untamed berry bushes and flower borders in various states of cultivation as the seasons change.

TIPS

· Always keep a seed sowing job ready for newcomers. A curious visitor is more likely to connect to the garden if they sow a few seeds. They'll want to come back to watch the seedlings grow. Fingers into soil, seeds into earth, creates a physical connection between person and the soil that is hard to shake. Conversely, asking a newcomer to pull weeds may not create the same connection. Keep some lettuce or radish seeds handy and a small planting bed empty, ready for new arrivals.

· Creating an atmosphere of inclusion is key to participation. A top-down hierarchy can put people off, especially those recently released from prison. Every idea is welcome, no matter how outlandish. Experienced gardeners need to keep an open mind and new gardeners need to consider traditional ideas. 'Let's give it a go and see what happens' is a great motto. Making mistakes, and learning from them, is all part of the growing experience.

· Every person is welcome no matter their ability, experience or personal history. It's all about here and now, while looking forward, working together to grow food for others.

· As we nurture plants in the garden, we also need to nurture each other, and ourselves, with the same care and attention. Patience is required as everything takes time to grow.

· Engaging former residents that still live in the area, who subscribe to the Incredible Edible ethos, to continue working in the garden provides consistency and facilitates the long term continuity of effort.

> 'LET'S GIVE IT A GO AND SEE WHAT HAPPENS' IS A GREAT MOTTO. MAKING MISTAKES, AND LEARNING FROM THEM, IS ALL PART OF THE GROWING EXPERIENCE.

MUTABBAL KOOSA
MIDDLE-EASTERN COURGETTE APPETIZER

This is great for garden picnics, served at room temperature with hummus, falafel and pita bread.

· 4 tbsp olive oil
· 1 small head of garlic, peeled and sliced (not a clove, a whole bulb of garlic)
· 650g courgettes, cut into 1/4 inch thick slices
· 4 tbsp good-tasting wine vinegar
· salt and pepper to taste
· 2 tbsp chopped spring onions
· a pinch of cayenne powder
· 2 tbsp finely chopped fresh coriander

Heat oil in a frying pan and sauté garlic slices over medium heat until they turn light brown. Remove garlic slices with a slotted spoon and set aside.
In the same oil, adding more if necessary, sauté courgette slices in batches over medium heat until they turn light brown, turning them over once. They won't be crisp. Remove and drain on paper towels. Combine vinegar with remaining ingredients.
Place courgette slices on a serving platter or into a container. Sprinkle vinegar mixture over top, then evenly top with garlic slices. Allow to stand for 4 hours or so before serving or taking to a picnic.

STORIES

In a lot of ways, the Incredible Edible focus solves many of the past challenges of this garden.

Previously the two main problems have been participation and direction. Most residents only stay at the facility for a few weeks and those days are filled with finding permanent accommodation, renewing relationships, and building a new post-prison life. For most, garden work isn't on their radar. However, there are many hours of down time spent in the grounds of the premises and having something to do helps pass the time productively. A loose but welcoming atmosphere in the garden means everyone is welcome at any time.

The general direction of "let's grow some food to share with others" provides an incentive to participate in activity that has meaning and a higher, altruistic purpose. Although they may not be there to harvest, a resident knows the seeds they sow today will be harvested by someone else and the produce given to others. Former residents, along with facility staff, help guide the general direction and provide consistency as residents hand over tasks. Problems in the garden are pointed out to curious residents and their imagination takes over for creative solutions. Tasks aren't assigned; opportunities are identified; creativity is encouraged.

As many of the gardeners have been of advanced years, through the generosity of Incredible Edible, we've built a number of chest-high raised beds to enable the participation of those who have trouble bending. These are sown with quick growing salad leaves, herbs and the like so residents can taste results within the few weeks of their residency.

The gardeners grow food to donate to food banks as well as seeing some of the fruits of their own labour in the meals served to the residents. Additionally they have helped out other Incredible Edible garden efforts by raising seedlings in our greenhouses to distribute to other area projects.

The garden offers a change in thinking. Instead of surviving day to day in the prison system, residents can feel a part of a greater society, by simply growing food to share with others in the community who may be struggling. Despite the security implications of post-prison life, residents can feel a sense of connection with others and a social responsibility that goes beyond the legal system. Incredible Edible gardening provides a sense of purpose, whether a sense of accomplishment for completing a daily task, or the larger notion of growing food to share.

Instead of the 'me against the world' mentality, by gardening, with the express purpose of helping others, residents are making a strong connection with the outside world. While this may seem like a small accomplishment, this subtle change in thinking contributes to reducing reoffending and the negative impact crime has on society. From a business perspective, volunteering in this garden gives ex-offenders their first reference on their new post-prison CV. It helps employers think positively about giving an ex-offender their first post-prison job. In a sense, this garden also grows new employees for local businesses.

APPROVED PREMISES

BARNET

ENGLAND

WHERE

Barnet is a north London suburb with lots of green spaces, both in public places and back gardens. To give an idea, it's roughly equivalent to Iceland in both size and population. Around 33% of the borough is protected green land, another 5% is public parks, and the majority of households have their own garden. The soil in London is typically clay and temperatures average around 5°C in the winter and up to 30°C in the summer. It rains all year round, generally around 60mm per month. Under the USDA Hardiness Zone rating Barnet is in zone 9.

WHO

Incredible Edible Barnet was set up by Wendy Alcock in 2016 when she ran out of room to grow food in her back garden. With a small group of volunteers, fruit, vegetables and edible flowers are grown outside a church (with a previous plot in a pub car park). Anyone in the community is welcome to pick them. Volunteers, including both experienced gardeners and first time growers wanting to learn how to grow some of their own food, cultivate a plot of land around 40 square metres on a shoestring budget. Each spring the group also holds a community seed swap where gardeners from Barnet and beyond are able to gather to swap seeds, plants and stories for free.

WHAT

The main community garden has a mixture of typical annual vegetables that can be grown in the UK such as tomatoes and courgettes. The plot also includes lots of perennials so there is some structure in the garden over winter. This includes herbs such as sage and mint. Fruit includes strawberries, and even a peach tree, which does well so far, despite the cold wet winters. The group like to grow plants that give multiple harvests and that people can easily grow at home. One of their goals is to show people what growing food organically in the UK looks like, which helps to raise awareness of the environmental, nutritional and health benefits of home growing.

STORIES

Until 2020 Incredible Edible Barnet only grew food in public places for people to see and share. But during the Covid-19 pandemic a dedicated group of volunteers realised fresh fruit and vegetables were going to be hard for some people in their community to reach. So Covid took them behind the gates of an allotment too. After a few emails to local allotments, in a matter of weeks, they were growing on several allotment plots in the borough and by the summer, they were harvesting food to take to a range of food banks and community centres in their neighbourhood. They also collected surplus food from other allotment holders on the site. In total, 600 kilos of fresh food was donated to their community. The allotments were only temporary but since then the group have added some new raised beds to the main growing space that are dedicated to food bank produce.

An aim for 2021 was to make the community garden, and food growing in general, more accessible to people from ethnic minorities. Barnet is very multicultural so it seemed important to grow more culturally diverse food plants for people to harvest locally. The group planted amaranth and chickpeas, as well as several squash plants such as dudi, achocha, and sharks' fin melon. They also shared the seeds with other community gardens in the area so others could enjoy the plants and food in different parts of the borough.

"GROW WHAT YOU AND YOUR COMMUNITY LOVE TO EAT, AND LEARN TO LOVE YOUR WEEDS! MANY OF THEM ARE EDIBLE TOO!

DELUXE PESTO FOR SNOBS

· 100g fresh basil
· 50g grated parmesan cheese
· 50g pine nuts, lightly toasted is best but not essential
· 1 medium clove of garlic, crushed
· 1 small pinch of salt, optional
· 100 - 150ml of olive oil

Blend the basil, parmesan, pine nuts, garlic and salt until it's a paste. Then mix in the olive oil until you get the consistency you like. That's it! Simply add to the dish of your choice and enjoy.

EVERYDAY PESTO FOR SNOBS

Basil is the common leaf used to make this dish originating in Genoa in Italy but any leaf with a strong flavour will make a delicious and quick sauce for pasta, bread, salad or lots of other dishes. Try fennel, nasturtium, rocket, coriander, kale, wild garlic or anything else you've got growing on your plot. You can also replace the pine nuts (walnuts, sunflower seeds or almonds are all delicious), cheese (try feta, cheddar or gouda) and oil (for example rapeseed, almond or avocado oil). For a vegan version replace the cheese with more nuts or add in a couple of tablespoons of nutritional yeast instead. Basically anything goes.

The recipe makes around 400ml of pesto which can be used straight away or frozen (in an ice cube tray if you have one) for a couple of months.

Wendy promises, once you've made your own home-made pesto from home-grown produce you will never look back. And you could even turn into a pesto snob like her!

TIPS

- Don't jump at the first plot of land you're offered – it's better to take a little time to make sure it will suit the needs of your group. Incredible Edible Barnet ditched their first plot in the pub car park because it was poor soil and hard to access. Hindsight suggested their efforts would have been better placed at the start making more links with the community to see where the plot would work best.

- Try something new each year.

- Ask for plants, seeds and equipment. A few donations will go a long way to getting you started. It's amazing how many people have an old unused compost bin, water butt or container taking up room in their garden.

- Winter (in temperate zones) was given to us for a reason – it's a great time for some rest while you restock your reserves for the burst of energy needed in spring.

- Get set up to stay in touch with your supporters as quickly as you can. An email list and social media accounts will set you off to a good start. You don't need to post and email often but they allow people to contact you and you to shout about all the great things you're getting up to.

- Label as many of your edible plants as you can so passers-by know which ones they can try.

TIPS

- Reach out to other community growers in your area. A network of any size will inspire you when things get tough and encourage you to keep growing.

- Make space to grow purple sprouting broccoli (Brassica oleracea var. italica) on your plot. It will take almost a year from seed to plate but it's well worth the wait. Also, it's a great tool to talk about food waste as no one who's grown it will want to waste a mouthful.

- If you're after a lower maintenance garden check out forest gardening or food forests. There are lots of edible perennial plants that look and taste great as well as encouraging biodiversity into your garden.

- Invite people to use your compost bins. It'll provide more well needed organic matter for your plot for free.

- Save some of your own seeds, it's a great way to grow locally adapted plants and will save you money too.

- If you have access to a lot of land (either in one space or over several spaces) start small and add more when you have the capacity to take it on sustainably. This includes having enough regular volunteers and finances to buy the resources you need.

- Get involved with local and national campaigns if you can. In the UK Garden Organic, the Soil Association, and Sustain are a few of the useful organisations to follow and support.

Incredible Edible Barnet welcomes anyone in Barnet to help at the garden, or pick the fruits of the team's collective labour, regardless of whether they've worked on the plot or not. In addition they hold one main community event each year - a seed swap in early March. This takes place during a couple of hours where gardeners from Barnet and beyond gather to talk plants and, of course, the weather – they are gardeners after all! The first was a low key event (and quite cold because it was at one of their plots outdoors - brrrr), but afterwards they were given the use of an indoor community space to hold their annual get together. All seeds are welcome – half used packets of seeds that are sitting at the bottoms of peoples' seeds tins, free packets from the front of magazines, self-saved seeds that people have grown at home and small plants are also often on the swapping table. There's usually cake involved too of course!

COMMUNITY

Learning happens in many ways at Incredible Edible Barnet. Growers, new and old, are nurtured to learn new skills. Group sessions are held on topics like composting, making leaf mould, seed sowing and winter planting. There is support for other people or groups wanting to set up community growing spaces in the borough. Growing at home is encouraged by the sharing of information and advice to their social media followers and mailing list. The team are always keen to go and visit as many different types of community garden as they can – including other Incredible Edible 'sibling' sites nearby. Learning from the experience of others is a really good way to find a gardening style that suits any space or place.

LEARNING

Building links with local businesses in their community is an important part of Incredible Edible Barnet's work. Following the permaculture ethics of "earth share, fair share and people care" any local organisation that uses one or more of these guiding values has the full support of the growing team. Local stores, such as the family run nursery and zero waste florist, often feature on the facebook page and a pick up point in Barnet for a local organic veg bag scheme has been set up. The group also links with other projects interested in nature based or environmental projects, as well as supporting the terrific but demanding work going on in the area's food banks by promoting them to their followers and donating food where possible.

BUSINESS

BARNET

BEESTON
ENGLAND

WHERE

Beeston is a great place to live. Situated next to the University of Nottingham and close to the Queen's Medical Centre, it attracts people from all over the world. The town has a real personality and strong community – many of the walls in Beeston are covered in beautiful street art – a project funded by the residents of Beeston. The town is thriving with many local and independent shops, restaurants and cafes. There is a huge selection of clubs and groups to be part of in Beeston. It's also situated next to Attenborough Nature Reserve which was recently purchased by Nottinghamshire Wildlife Trust thanks to grants, donations and publicity from the wonderful Sir David Attenborough.

WHO

In about 2019, we, Rose Harvey, Jack Horner, Rosanna Wilson, Ian Coleman, Heather Sarno, Lily Cameron, Cheryl Nicklin and Shaun Dannheimer, set up our first site. We have since recruited more volunteers and have a WhatsApp group of volunteers for each site where volunteers can ask, 'who's nipping down to water the plants?' if it hasn't rained for a while, or 'who's replacing the watering can that's broken?'

WHAT

We started off with a small patch of land. We began digging, planted some edible plants (broad beans, onions, courgettes, potatoes...) and put up a small sign saying 'Incredible Edible Beeston.' In 2020 we asked if we could do the same thing in some local parks. We now have 3 additional sites - 2 in local parks next to playgrounds and 1 next to the tram line. In addition to what we started growing initially, we're now also growing kale, strawberries, peas, carrots, orach, rhubarb, apples, gooseberries, lettuce, tomatoes, cauliflower and more!

> **"JUST GET GOING. PEOPLE HAVE DIFFERENT STRENGTHS, CONTACTS, RESOURCES, AND ARE GENERALLY GOOD AND WANT TO HELP. ASK FOR IT WHEN YOU NEED IT AND YOU'LL SEE THAT THINGS WORK OUT."**

STORIES

We didn't really have any real permission to start the first site... we kind of just got on with it and thought "what's the worst that can happen?!" Then, I think the council saw we were looking after it and agreed to let us start some new sites. It's a great project and we always see families and dog walkers wandering over to the sites wondering why there are now peas and runner beans growing next to the playground! We have a wonderful group of regular volunteers for each site without whom the project would not be possible. We're so grateful for their support. We don't have any definite plans for the future - we're happy to let things grow organically. The main idea is just to get the conversation going about local food and to show people that actually we can be agents of change.

TIPS

· Ask for help – we've never had any funding, but every time we've needed something, we've asked on social media and the people of Beeston have never let us down.

· Use signage so people know the name of the project and how to get in touch.

· Invite Pam Warhurst for a talk. She is a force of nature. It is hugely inspirational to listen to her and pick up tips and ideas.

· Keep growing simple and make it visually striking if you can. For example, runner beans are incredibly easy to grow and beautiful when climbing & twisting up bamboo canes. Marigolds and sunflower seeds are edible and add a lot of beauty to the sites. Broad beans are easy and pop up early in the season so they're a great one to start off with then they can be replaced with tomatoes later in the summer.

· Work with a key group of people you can rely on – people who are willing to commit to regular sessions and to working behind the scenes. Draw on each other's strengths – one might be great at social media, another at growing.

· Don't take on more than you can handle and keep things simple.

· Never pressure volunteers. Don't ask people to do anything they don't want to do; if they can't turn up for a month / 2 months, that's fine! We appreciate anything people can do to help. We only want people to take part if they enjoy taking part.

· Explain why you are doing the project. When people understand the motivation for Incredible Edible it's easier for them to commit to it. For example, we recently shared a picture of a young girl picking some lettuce with the caption: "This is why we started the project. Because we believe in a future where local growing, strong communities and caring about the planet are the norm. Granted – our project won't change the world overnight, but it might help inspire people to push for change."

SEASONAL RAVIOLI

CREDIT TO BARNET FOR RECIPE AND PHOTOS

Makes 2 large or 3 small portions

· For the pasta:
· 200g of 00 (special Italian type of flour) or plain flour
· 2 eggs (or 100ml of water)
· Splash of olive oil

Prepare the filling (you're aiming for around 300g of mixture): Your choice of seasonal veg (softer ingredients give a nicer texture) eg. steamed beetroot in spring, wilted spinach in summer, fried mushrooms in autumn or roasted squash in winter. A handful of cheese like feta, ricotta or parmesan, or nutritional yeast and mustard for vegans. Anything else that complements your creation – herbs, nuts or dried fruit will give your dish a boost.

To make the pasta place a hole in the centre of the flour and fold in the egg (or water). Knead the mixture for around 5 minutes until smooth. Add a little oil or water if the dough is too stiff, but you don't want it to become too wet. Form into a ball, place in a plastic bag and refrigerate for at least 30 minutes.

Roll the dough. A pasta machine makes things easier but you can use a rolling pin, rolling a piece at a time. Thinner pasta will cook better: setting 5 or 6 on a pasta machine or 1-2mm if hand rolling. Dust the pasta with flour to prevent sticking.

There are gadgets for shaping ravioli; trays, rollers or presses, but a cookie cutter is fine, or even hand cut the dough and crimp the edges with your fingers or a fork.

Sandwich about 1 Tablespoon of filling between the pasta shapes and seal. This is the time consuming bit so don't leave it until 5 minutes before dinner to get started! Then, when you're ready to eat, add to boiling salted water for around 3-5 minutes and serve drizzled with oil and parmesan, or nutritional yeast.

A wonderful local illustrator made beautiful painted signs for each site and a skilled local lady made some planters for us with 'Incredible Beeston' written on the front. Whenever we're down at the site, passersby always comment on how lovely the project is. We're hoping to put some "help yourself" signs up and a chalk board with a list of what's ready to pick so it's obvious that the point is for the public to freely help themselves to the produce. So much has been donated by the public. When we've needed compost bins, plants, top soil etc we've just put a shout out on local media and the public have come to the rescue within days.

COMMUNITY

We regularly see parents watering the plants with their children. We'd love to see local schools with their own Incredible Edible planters in the playground and people taking more of an interest in growing. We're taking things step by step and hope to see a renewed interest in and respect for growing. A lady recently commented on Facebook: "My 2-year-old has been loving picking the strawberries, broad beans and mangetouts. It's something really lovely and fun to do together – plus it helps him try more veg which is always a plus! A fruit farm would overwhelm him so it's the perfect size for him! Thank you to all the volunteers for providing this fab project!"

LEARNING

We have been supported by local businesses. In the beginning we had some wood chip dropped off by a local tree surgeon and received donations of plants from The Beeston Gardening Community Facebook page. A local donut company 'DoughNotts' also contacted us asking if we would like them to raise some money for us. We said yes of course! They sold their "Bee-kind" donuts at the monthly Beeston Farmers' Market and were sold out by mid-morning! They raised £100 which went towards our liability insurance. We're currently in the process of contacting local businesses, restaurants and cafes to see if they are happy to have a planter with the Incredible Edible logo on it outside their location which then generates an appreciation for the businesses from local people . We'd love to have the project to grow into the wider community as it has in Todmorden!

BUSINESS

BEESTON

BURLEY IN WHARFEDALE
ENGLAND

WHERE

Burley-in-Wharfedale was first established in the 900s and sits on the northern edge of Bradford Metropolitan District Council in West Yorkshire in the north of England. During the Industrial Revolution water was drawn off the River Wharfe through a small man-made channel to power the cotton mills. Although the mills are long gone, this goit remains and today is used to generate hydro-electric power. The village has expanded enormously over the last one hundred years with many people working in the nearby cities of Leeds and Bradford. The village is a thriving community which offers a wide range of activities and interest groups for all ages.

WHO

We began Incredible Edible here in August 2020 in the teeth of the COVID epidemic. Penny Wright came up with the idea of a community herb garden to mark the fantastic support given by the people of Burley in Wharfedale to each other during the COVID pandemic. With support from the Parish Council and Community Trust, an overgrown bed was identified and transformed in the autumn by a group of volunteers, Philip Wright, Emma Mark, Margaret Watson and Jade Holdsworth.

WHAT

We have over 30 herbs which include both annuals and perennials with tips for their use written on slates and on our Facebook page. In the autumn of 2020, the chair of The Community Trust successfully applied for a small grant from the Shipley Community Chest for two additional vegetable beds to be built behind the library. At the height of summer 2021, these beds were bursting with all kinds of vegetables.

STORIES

At the original site we designed and built a four quadrant bed based on the points of the compass with a bay tree in the centre. Over the months the bed took shape and, as spring came, the garden began to flourish with herbs ready for picking. The response from so many people has been wonderful. In summer, we have a whole array of delicious herbs for use by anyone in the community. At first picking it was a little tentative but confidence is spreading by word of mouth and through social media.

We are very fortunate to have the original core group of enthusiastic volunteers with others pitching in when they are able. We also have great neighbours, with the issue of watering being overcome by the generosity of one local household offering use of their hosepipe and water, and another providing farmyard manure and slates for signs. We have had many plant and slate donations from villagers. As we knew quite a bit about herb growing but much less about vegetable growing we have been very pleased to accept advice from local "vegetable experts".

Village organisations have also been wonderfully helpful. The Parish Council offered us the original circular bed to create the garden. The Burley in Wharfedale Community Trust supported the project with some funding to clear the bed and supply building materials.

Our library set up a complimentary pilot project called Green Shoots in 2021 and plan to create a small accessible community garden in the library grounds primarily for education and learning. They had a launch day event in June 2021 in partnership with our Incredible Edible Community Herb Garden. This included family activities such as storytelling from Maddie Coelho of Story Bees, quizzes and trails, all on a gardening theme. Green Shoots has a small working group led by the library manager Abigail Skerrey and lead project volunteer Bev Plaxton.

We are learning on the job with advice from the Yorkshire and Humber Incredible Edible WhatsApp group, local experts, and, of course, some trial and error. For example, should we plant rhubarb for communal picking as the leaves can be poisonous? Following an alert from a man walking his dog, we discussed, researched and added the cautionary skull and crossbones sign to the bed. Although it would take more rhubarb leaves to poison someone than would fit in most wheelbarrows it was nonetheless a good lesson in awareness of public safety.

TIPS

· Don't be put off by people saying the beds will be vandalised, ours haven't been yet and if they were we would replant.

· Get your water supply sorted, water is heavy to carry any distance.

· Due to wonderful enthusiasm things may move faster than you anticipate so be prepared for the unexpected.

FINES HERBES OMELETTE WITH GREEN SALAD

As we are a Community Herb Garden a simple and delicious herb recipe seems appropriate. Herbs provide another dimension to what may be commonplace dishes. The classic *Fines Herbes* are parsley, French tarragon, chervil and chives, all of which grow in abundance in our garden. Our lunchtime menu comprises *Fines Herbes* omelette and a green salad washed down with ice cold water flavoured with ginger mint and alpine strawberries, decorated with borage and cornflower petals.

Omelette for 1 or 2
· Three eggs
· A good dollop of butter
· Salt and pepper
· A handful of chopped *Fines Herbes* (French tarragon, flat leaved parsley, chervil, chives)
Beat the eggs and season with salt and pepper.
Add half of the herbs to the mix.
Melt the butter in a small frying pan at low to medium heat until foaming but not browning.
Add the egg mix and swirl around to cover the whole pan.
Let the mixture cook for about 30 seconds and then using a spatula or similar move the mix around a little to allow the runny mix to fill up the gaps created.
Do this one or two times more until the egg mix is nearly set.
Sprinkle the other half of the *Fines Herbes* across the top of the mix.
Tilt the pan and flip the top half of the omelette across the bottom half, or use a spatula to fold it over.
Slide onto a warm plate.

Green salad with Classic French Dressing
For a salad, using whatever greens you have available, add a little of any of the following: lovage, buckler-leaved sorrel, basil, garden mint, nasturtium, fennel (torn)
dill, flat leaved parsley, chives, chervil, french tarragon (chopped).
To make one jar:
· Half a teaspoon of Dijon mustard and a pinch of salt
· Half a teaspoon of runny clear honey
· One tablespoon red wine vinegar
· One tablespoon extra virgin olive oil
· Two tablespoons vegetable oil
Put the salt, mustard and honey into a jam jar and mix together. Stir in the vinegar. Add the oils and screw the lid of the jar on. Shake hard until you have made an emulsion. Toss the salad with the dressing.

SEEING YOU BUILD AND TEND THE HERB GARDEN HAS BROUGHT RAY SO MUCH PLEASURE. HE FEELS LIKE A GUARDIAN TO THE BED AND WATCHES OVER IT WHEN YOU ARE NOT AROUND.

In July 2021 one of the Brownie packs visited the herb garden to plant Alpine Strawberries and sampled the delights of the garden. Since then they have brought their families along to enjoy the garden. We are attending and contributing information and herb posies to the Community Trust stall at the Burley Summer Festival in August. This will give us the opportunity to reach out to and get involved with other groups and individuals as we begin to 'break out' from the pandemic. The library is a regular partner and through them, the Parish Council, and the Community Trust, we hope we will build up links with other local organisations, schools and village initiatives. As time goes on we can see the potential for many projects of mutual benefit.

50%

COMMUNITY

We are very lucky to have a national horticultural expert living in the village, David Allison, who, amongst other things, is the Royal Horticultural Society Vice Chairman of their Fruit, Vegetable and Herb plant committee. He has provided us with support, information and plants from his allotments. We have been able to learn from him as he has kindly given us time regularly. Our small group of volunteers is expanding. We meet once a month for a regular weed and review of the beds. This provides us with on-the-job learning that goes both ways.

40%

LEARNING

As we have been established less than a year it's too soon to say how what we are doing may lead to income generation, or how it will contribute to the economic success of our local businesses or the community at large. Our sense is that Incredible Edible is a uniting force and that our version of it can only further cement an already close-knit community.

10%

BUSINESS

BURLEY IN WHARFEDALE

CAMBERWELL
ENGLAND

WHERE

The Thorlands Estate, in Camberwell, in the London Borough of Lambeth has 400 dwelling units in low rise flats and is home to thousands of people. The wider area of Camberwell is in south London with Georgian and Victorian buildings, juxtaposed with many social housing estates, theatre, gallery and museums and has a long historical connection with the arts, which includes Camberwell College of Arts.

WHO

Thorlands Gardens is a club run by Simon J Taylor, a London based garden consultant, who specialises in design and management of food and ecological systems. In 2019 he initiated the project with John Frankland, the Chairman of the Thorlands Housing Management Society (THMS). Simon and three members of the THMS initiated the gardens club with a soft launch at a seasonal gathering, with some residents in December 2019. At a subsequent residents' meeting the project, and Simon's tenureship, gained the mandate needed to begin. Work started almost immediately in February 2020. By 2021 over sixty individuals were signed-up, equally split between residents and non-residents. Some are parent - child attendees. Others are young, some are middle aged and some are much older. There are ten or more regular attendees, with a spattering of occasional attendees and newcomers in the mix.

WHAT

There is land of 1.2 acres with about half of that now being under cultivation or regeneration. The garden spaces are unique and also diverse. The Walled Garden and The Forest Food Garden produce green vegetables, root crops, beans, soft fruits, herbs, edible flowers and potted plants for our own use and for sale. The old rent office is where Thorlands Gardens Club holds small meetings, keeps an office, a kitchenette and a storeroom for tools. The Clubhouse Garden outside, as yet unfenced, will have a terrace extension and already has its very own kitchen garden mainly full with herbs, flowers for insects, and medicinal plants. It's ripe for a design created by the volunteers.

"WE HAVE DEVELOPED A COST ANALYSIS ARGUMENT ON THE USE OF OUR UNCULTIVATED .6 ACRES. IF WE LOOK BEYOND AN IMMEDIATE CASH RETURN, AND CONSIDER THE DANGERS OF FOOD SECURITY AND THE COSTS OF POOR MENTAL HEALTH, WE CAN SEE THAT ACCESS TO GREEN SPACES AND QUALITY FRESH FOOD PAYS. PERSUADING PEOPLE OF THIS NEW METRIC IS OUR GREATEST ACHIEVEMENT.

ELDERFLOWER FRITTERS

Credit to Simon J. Taylor and his book, *Growing Pot to Cooking Pot*.

I remember this recipe from being a young child in the Gloucestershire Cotswolds, 'Laurie Lee Country'. Whenever I make them I am launched into a mess of emotional nostalgia for the singing of the skylark and the beauty of the Cotswold escarpment hills and poetic views.

Use unpolluted newly ripe florets sourced from a bush far from a road. Flowers come into their prime slowly when in shade, unmolested by beetles and aphids. Sniff. If floral, that's good. Slightly smelling of socks or petrochemicals and they are no good at all.

Serves 4-6
· 6 medium (or 3 large) Elderflower florets
· 250ml dairy milk or plant milk
· 6 heaped dessert spoons strong white flour or equivalent wheat free. Vegan versions need a stiffer, yet still creamy, batter using a little extra flour
· 2 large eggs or equivalent volume of vegan soft cheese
· 2 heaped tsp honey or 3 tsp white sugar (brown sugars inhibit elderflower flavour)
· 1 or 2 grinds of sea salt or rock salt
· ½ teaspoon of bicarbonate of soda
· Splash of fizzy lager or sparkling mineral water
· 50g of butter or 3-4 tablespoons of vegetable oil (for batter)
· 500ml of vegetable oil

Method
Mix all but the florets and oil in a medium size ceramic or glass bowl as metal can effect the flavour. Ensure all lumps are removed.
When bubbles are forming and popping it's good to go.
In a deep pan pre-heat the oil for a few minutes on a high heat. Test with a teaspoon of batter, gently releasing it into the fat. The batter should bubble, if it browns in mere seconds, reduce the heat slightly. The fritters need to be golden brown on the outside and cooked through on the inside. One by one thoroughly coat the florets in batter. Drip off the excess and place in the oil, turning regularly. Let cook to a light to medium golden brown, remove, and place on tissue to absorb the excess fat. The texture should be crispy like Japanese tempura. Remove bits of batter from the oil and top up as needed. Serve while still warm with dairy or vegan cream or ice-cream.

STORIES

The Walled Garden is where we had our first sessions. It used to be an old unloved, walled and fenced, tarmacked sports cage called the 'Kick-a-Bout' and was abused, vandalised, and marked by undesirable behaviour. We had to clear tons of scrub, and repurpose three previously built raised beds. In two sessions, six or seven of us had it cleared. We filled about four ton bags, as well as making piles of green and brown compost. In three further sessions two of the raised beds were repurposed and one was left as a 'signature bed.' The former were turned into wall troughs and two became one metre square beds on legs. This 270 square metre space is now half way through its metamorphosis into a space with many more beds and troughs with about 110 square metres of growing space, including different examples of vertical growing. It now houses a potting shed partly made with international pallets. It also has a see-through polythene roof for shelter. Attached is a lovely re-purposed antique oak pergola. We hope soon this will be covered with honeysuckle and grapevines.

The Forest Food Garden is adjacent. The idea here is to use the existing scrub bushes to create a medium level canopy under the canopy of the major trees. This space is about six hundred square metres, is full of flowers (weeds!), and has years of leaf mould as a carpet for growing new useful, edible, trees and shrubs. We already have a 'pet' blackberry bush moulded into a ball shape for easy prickle-free picking! This garden has two or three tricks up its sleeve. In a former life it was a wooden-style adventure playground. A hidden sports platform, which can be discovered under bushes, constructed out of railway sleepers, is right up against the Walled Garden next door and provides a perfect place to create a doorway connection between the two sides. The plan for this area is to re-purpose it as a place for events, including outdoor theatre, music and arts. And a stage!

There are other tricks, not so secret, or rather not secret now, as they too were covered in brambles and brush before. One, being an old metal swing frame over a rubberised flooring. This 120 square metre space will surely be our seated hammock and yoga area! Lastly and by no means least, the third space is a 250 square metres hard terrace with high wall on two sides providing shelter from the prevailing wind. The terrace in the Forest Food Garden is the perfect area for a market event, which indeed is earmarked!

The Clubhouse Garden is an area not yet developed but offers a social space for coffee mornings, afternoon tea, and particularly for residents to drop-in to socialise. Indeed it has the potential to be a great hospitality terrace for special events. The idea here is to encourage more people to engage in the gardens and volunteer, as well as attract more experienced growers with skills and entrepreneurial spirit.

   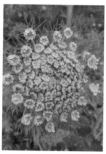 

TIPS

· Land ownership in London can be complex. Leases and ancient land-rights belonging to the Crown or the Church, notwithstanding legal agreements between them and estates, tenants, housing associations and local authorities, can make acquiring permission to grow daunting. Do your best to find out who you need to approach so that you are dealing with the right organisation as soon as possible.

· In London, making friends with Incredible Edible groups in your adjoining boroughs is a valuable asset when trying to navigate ownership rights.

· Network, network, network, seeking partners all of the time.

· Do your research so as to limit funding failures.

· Take your time - get the legal structures/ agreements in place.

· Find the right people to work with.

The great space we have at our disposal, and its varied nature, attracts a wide church. Additionally, Thorlands Gardens Club itself offers regular workshop-style sessions, advertising them to residents and non-residents alike using seasonal posters and e-flyers, via social media and email, as well as news-updates and reminders.

A traditional workshop with two rooms, one for clean work and one messy, to make dust, is where we did most of the build for The Walled Garden. It's perfect for bad weather and ready and waiting for keen wood-working and do-it-yourself enthusiasts.

Plenty of produce benefits residents and local volunteers, from compost, pots and plants to grow at home on the window ledge, to fresh organic produce to embellish any meal. These benefits have positively impacted residents and non-residents, with a sense of pride, wellbeing, and belonging. Probably the most important of all, which is often mentioned, is a sense of being safer!

35% COMMUNITY

Our training program trained two interns in 2021-2 into paid part-time positions to assist in the garden and running the market stall. This program is being extended and will run annually with increasing numbers.

35% LEARNING

We part-fund the project by re-investing onsite sales of herbs, plants and flowers to buy seeds, sundries, and to pay wages and have two market stalls one of which is on site. A third weekly stall with a paid stall keeper is in plan. A local pub chef is developing an autumn menu highlighting our zero miles produce.

The Clubhouse Garden sells teas and coffees and is a social space for the area, ticking both the box for community and also enterprise.

Some discussion has already taken place around market gardening work on site. With careful planning we can increase the amount of food, herbs, flowers and potted plants we grow. A partnership agreement to share with the Thorlands estate to provide an income stream back to the residents is in plan. It's an embryonic step toward social enterprise, local employment creation, and is a mini-example of community wealth building.

30% BUSINESS

CAMBERWELL

CERGY-PONTOISE
FRANCE

WHERE

Cergy-Pontoise, a new town made up of thirteen districts. It is situated 30km north-west of Paris and has welcomed various Incredible Edible groups since 2012.

WHO

Today, around 20 groups tend vegetable plots and planters. These are indicated on a street map of the area. It is updated each year for participants and visitors and available from the town's tourist office in Pontoise.

WHAT

The Incredible Edible gardens include a vegetable plot under the windows of the Préfecture government office building, a footpath border leading to the railway station in Pontoise, and an experimental garden located in the grounds of a listed building, the former weekend retreat of French actor, Gérard Philipe.

"WE REMEMBER THE POWER OF SMALL ACTIONS! THANKS TO PAM WARHURST!

HOP HERBAL TEA

To make herbal tea, pick a handful of hop flowers when in full bloom in September or early October. Spread them out to dry in a well-aired place or in a cool oven. Infuse well in a litre of boiled water, strain and sweeten with honey. Traditionally hop tea is used as a diuretic or sipped in the evening to ensure a good night's sleep. The taste will depend on the variety of hops used.

STORIES

The work we have done has travelled in that in 2016 six people from South Korea came to Cergy, representing Seoul and their parks department. Their visit was entirely to learn more about Incredible Edible and growing food in towns.

Since 2018, Incredible Edible planters have embellished the 4-metre high urban chicken coop next to a retirement home and provided food for four hens together with scraps donated by local inhabitants. Faced with a glut of dry bread brought by residents, unsuitable for the hens, Noël and Gillian Constans looked to recycle it. They contacted Colin Smith of the local brewery, Hake Brew, to turn it into beer. With the help of volunteers from *Alternativ* Network, who collected the bread, Colin was able to brew *La Bidule* in June 2020, a locally sourced bread beer, consumed locally. A second brew is in preparation for summer 2021 using different varieties of hops grown on Incredible Edible plots around Cergy-Pontoise and wild hops growing near the river Oise.

50%

COMMUNITY

Incredible Edible Cergy Pontoise takes part in local events such as national Gardens Day, organises workshops open to all, and picnics on garden plots. *Points communs* from the theatre in Cergy joined with Incredible Edible to cultivate a vegetable garden next to the theatre. Potted plants were included in a green exhibition in the theatre last year. As a result some of their employees have become active gardeners.

40%

LEARNING

Students of English and others have visited the garden in the town centre during classes. One teacher organized a botanical treasure hunt involving 30 different plant varieties which students photographed.

10%

BUSINESS

Using bread donated to the chicken run and bread collected from local canteens, hospitals and bakers' shops, together with local hops, we had a hand in *La Bidule*, a locally sourced bread beer that was brewed in 2020 and launched in March 2020. A further semi-commercial collaboration was set up with the university to help out with garden tools, meeting rooms and developing a seed bank. In return Incredible Edible helps cultivate their terrace garden.

CERGY–PONTOISE

COMMUNITY GARDENS AUSTRALIA AUSTRALIA

WHERE

Australia is the world's sixth largest country. Like Canada, despite its size, it has a relatively small population of less than 30M. The interior is largely arid, and the country as a whole has very low rainfall of under 500mm, with increasing occurrences of extreme weather events including flooding and wildfires. Rainforests, mountains, wetlands, temperate, tropical and semi-tropical conditions provide for a wide variety of growing conditions and contribute to its huge range of biodiversity.

WHO

Community Gardens Australia (CGA) exists to nurture, support and advocate for community gardening activities all over Australia. This entirely volunteer run organisation has a network of eager regional representatives. These operate as a 2 way conduit between the organisation's management committee and the actual community gardens themselves. Their website contains an extensive set of resources, collated and designed to encourage and support all types of community gardening initiatives. They spend a great deal of time working towards better policy development at the local level, and furthering support for community gardening activities.

WHAT

CGA has over 500 gardens listed in their rapidly expanding online directory and estimates that there could easily be up to another 1000 or more around the country. That doesn't take into account the 2000+ Stephanie Alexander school kitchen gardens, verge gardens, community food forests and orchards as well as guerrilla gardens that are popping up all over the place. The fact is, Australians are mad for urban food growing and CGA is there to support that madness in as many ways as they can!

> **"IT'S PRETTY CLEAR THAT THERE IS A ROLE FOR GOVERNMENT TO PROVIDE THE SUPPORT NEEDED FOR COMMUNITY GARDENS, AS THEY MIGHT PROVIDE SUPPORT FOR ANY OTHER HEALTH AND WELLBEING INITIATIVES."**

TIPS

- Don't get hung up on names. We get it that Community Gardens Australia is not Incredible Edible. That doesn't take away from our shared vision and our shared goals which are all about connecting people through food and using food as the springboard into making changes for a more fair and kind society.

- Never underestimate the value of having high profile individuals batting for you.

STORIES

Throughout 2020, some community gardens were forced to close during COVID lockdowns. CGA and their partner organisations helped cut through the bureaucracy and assist gardeners to regain access. President of CGA, Naomi Lacey, was able to point out at the time, "when it comes to transmitting infection, visiting your local community garden to gather food is less dangerous than going to the supermarket." However, many local authorities did amazing work to support gardens to stay open so that people could access the food they had been growing, even with all the restrictions in place. Some authorities even took over the watering of the gardens to reduce the need for people to be out and about and potentially spreading the virus.

The profile and value of what is being done in Australia has already achieved some recognition. Naomi Lacey and Gavin Hardy of CGA, in 2019 and 2020 respectively, were both awarded Churchill Fellowships to study other community garden networks and community food forestry around the globe. Although stalled in their travels by COVID, Naomi and Gavin have nonetheless used their time to make strong connections with people world-wide. For Naomi this has included a number of conversations with Pam Warhurst, chair of Incredible Edible CIC.

It's pretty clear that there is a role for the Australian Government to provide the support needed for community gardens in Australia, just as they might provide support for any other health and wellbeing initiative. One need only look at the success of the Australian Men's Shed Association, with its 1000+ sheds all over Australia and its fantastic record of supporting men's mental health, to know that something like growing food in communities can touch the lives of everyone - men, women and children of all ages - will be a good thing. It is well known that community gardens are hugely beneficial for ALL of the population, whatever anyone's age or ability. So, CGA will be looking to the Australian Government to recognise both how widespread and how influential their movement is and can be. Once this recognition is there, the expectation is that this will be followed up with funding to support their efforts as currently the organisation is managed entirely by volunteers.

BANANA AND COCONUT CHUTNEY

· 1 tbsp brown mustard seeds
· ¼ cup white vinegar
· 1 ½ cups shredded or desiccated coconut
· 1 cup water
· ¾ cup white vinegar
· 1 ¼ cup vegetable oil
· 1 onion, finely chopped
· 3 cloves garlic, crushed
· 4 tsp grated fresh ginger
· 12 fresh red chillies, chopped
· 2 tsp chilli powder
· 1 tbsp cumin
· 2 tbsp turmeric
· 2 medium tomatoes, chopped
· 1.2kg ripe bananas, chopped
· ¾ cup firmly packed brown sugar
· Salt
· 1 tbsp lime juice
· ¼ cup fresh coriander, chopped

Combine mustard seeds and ¼ cup vinegar in glass bowl, stand overnight.

Combine coconut with water and extra vinegar in bowl. Cover, stand 1 hour.

Heat oil in pan, add onion, garlic, chilli, chilli powder, cumin and turmeric. Cook, stirring until fragrant.

Add tomatoes. Cook, stirring until softened.

Stir in mustard seed mixture and bananas. Simmer, uncovered, stirring occasionally until thick.

Stir in sugar and coconut mixture. Simmer, uncovered, stirring occasionally for further 10 minutes or until mixture is thickened slightly.

Stir in remaining ingredients.

Pour into hot, sterilised jars. Seal while hot.

Makes about 7 cups.

CGA knows that gardening offers huge benefits to individuals but is even more aware of the fact that gardening with others, and specifically growing food and sharing it with others, has multiple, well documented outcomes for people. CGA helped to promote the 2020 Pandemic Gardening Survey conducted by Sustain: The Australian Food Network. Results clearly showed that of the 9,140 respondents 72% felt that their gardening activities had either significantly or greatly benefitted their mental health and wellbeing during the pandemic and that for 81% of respondents gardening had contributed a sense of focus and reduced anxiety. CGA is well aware that it has been very difficult for people during lockdowns when they have had to miss out on their regular community gardening activities with others.

And that's because community is what it's all about. Us humans need that contact with others whilst engaging in meaningful activities to make us feel more alive and truly connected. To have opportunities that help us know that we are not alone, and to be able to share the experience of living with each other as well as being connected with nature whilst having access to nourishing food, is at the heart of community gardening for many people.

CGA has already demonstrated on a small scale the health benefits which extend throughout the community. They have identified that up-skilling, advice and training for community gardeners is universally sought. CGA is working to collaborate with partner organisations to provide comprehensive training opportunities around the country. They are also developing a whole bunch of resources as well as updating older ones that are available on their website for free. Along with increasing their social media presence and utilising their celebrity ambassadors they hope to grow awareness of community gardening throughout Australia.

The scope of organisations like CGA to have an impact on communities, on learning, and on enterprise is huge. Increasingly, in a world where reducing carbon emissions is now critical, encouraging people to eat locally and grow more of their own food helps to lower food miles and support local businesses and growers. Nowhere is this more demonstrable than in Australia whose urban populations border the coasts and are separated by vast kilometres of roads where food is transported from one end of the country to the other. The business benefits of localising food systems include lower costs, fresher food and therefore improved custom which then feeds back into the community through lower traffic pollution, better diets and all of their attendant health consequences. A move away from centralised supermarket models, even if just in tiny steps, improves the elastic strength of community and its capacity to adapt to changing environmental circumstances such as floods, wildfires and plagues of vermin, which Australia has been experiencing to a heightened extent in recent years.

CONWY TOWN

WALES

WHERE

Conwy Town is an ancient settlement on the coast of North Wales. The building of town and castle dates from the 1280s. The walled city is much visited since it has the most extensive intact medieval walls in Europe and was recently recognised as a World Heritage Site. The graceful and more modern Thomas Telford suspension bridge, completed in 1826, links pedestrians from both sides of the River Conwy and is in the care of The National Trust, Britain's foremost conserver of buildings, monuments, gardens and landscapes. Churches, beaches, and even the smallest house in Britain, continue to attract visitors at all times of the year.

WHO

In 2013, Ruth Bitowski spied 36 decking squares from a skip, hauled them out, and was inspired to make her idea of an Incredible Edible group in Conwy Town a reality. She contacted Jane Hughes, who had some responsibility for Gwledd Conwy Feast, to see about having a fledgling Incredible Edible as something new at this annual food festival. Founded in the early 2000s, the Feast is a local food festival helping local food producers to showcase their products with some even finding their way into shops as prestigious as Harrods in London. Celia Williams became involved and posters went up in Conwy Town to invite people to take part in establishing a local Incredible Edible. At the first meeting in 2013, thirty people came to support the idea, including Mary Pugh who has been a dedicated and constant member ever since. New residents Gayle and Chris Brace joined a year later and through their involvement have found an enduring network of friends. Cath and Mike Mosey joined in 2017 and have helped formalise the activities while Trefor Price, who also joined in 2017, has become a backbone of our many activities.

WHAT

We started with apples and a few herbs. We quickly realised that trees need space larger than a mere planter and we worked with the local orchard group to establish more apple trees before concentrating on growing vegetables. We have learned from Incredible Edible in Todmorden that vegetables grown above the ground are more visible to the public. So our summer focus is on many types of beans, courgettes, sweet corn, peas, lettuce, raspberries, currants, strawberries (provided the birds don't get to them first!), with winter crops including plenty of brassicas and kale. All of these are both readily recognised and easy to pick. Amidst them we ensure that there are plenty of insect and bee-friendly flowers.

STORIES

Any challenges we had before the pandemic have faded into insignificance. When people's lives were and still are at stake, staying safe became the single most important thing we could all do. As many of the beds were owned by institutions we were not allowed to tend the gardens as a group. But during daily exercise, either individually or in family bubble, we would walk past the beds and pull a few weeds out here and there. Facebook messages from the public showed us that people appreciated being able to help themselves to the herbs. This spurred us on.

The Toll House garden, next to the suspension bridge, is owned by the National Trust. During the pandemic National Trust rules prevented us from gardening. Watching that garden become overgrown again was heart breaking. Yet from probably one of the worst situations imaginable in 2020 sprang forth the best. Sharing and kindness is the name of our game, and so we started to think up ways in which this could be achieved differently. Then it happened by the bucket load...

We began delivering spare vegetable plants to those who were shielding and self-isolating. We supplied Cath and Mike's garden gate stall, which arrived right when it was needed the most. We gave hundreds of plants away as shops emptied of anything seedy, green or grow-able. Community members connected over growing food. Spare produce went to the food bank as the normal practice of picking the harvest by anyone receded. Our project #Stay at Home and Grow Your Own brought us UK Lottery funding so we could pull out all the stops to get seed and compost giveaways organised. We found ourselves doing lots of seed counting, stuffing envelopes with seeds, bagging compost, and printing labels and instructions. 150 packs were distributed to those self isolating, shielding and two families with school children all wanting to grow their own at home. We felt no doubts at all about being able to pull it off and we did, all within three weeks!

In 2021, creating safe environments to work in has been a challenge. Gardens can only be worked if there are risk assessments with COVID precautions in place – making sure there are cleaning stations available with hand sanitizer, disinfectant sprays and wipes. We check with members to make sure they feel safe in the working environment. We ask if they are happy to do that particular job in that area. Many bring their own hand tools to help create a feeling of safety. Safe people are happy people.

APPLE CIDER VINEGAR, ACV

CREDIT TO VINITA RAMKOLOWON

ACV is credited all over the Internet but for real health benefits it should be raw and organic, which can be costly. Yet this wonderful resource is so simple to make using very few ingredients. During lockdown several of us made it. Despite face pulling due to tartness, the different tastes were surprising. Any combination of varieties can be used, which definitely has an impact on flavour.

Ingredients
· organic apple pieces/scraps - crab apples add flavour
· 8 tbsp raw cane sugar
· 2.5 litres water, filtered or boiled and cooled
· 3-4 sterilised glass bottles with lids
· Cheesecloth or coffee filter paper
· A rubber band

Method
Clean and air dry a gallon jar.
Fill the jar ¾ full with scraps or roughly chopped apples.
Dissolve the sugar in 500ml of the water.
Pour over the apples until submerged.
Add the rest of the water ensuring apples are covered.
Weigh down the fruit using a small glass. Exposed apples may turn mouldy.
Cover with cheesecloth/coffee filter paper secured with a rubber band.
Store in a dark place at room temperature.
After 3 weeks, it will smell sweet but not vinegary.
Strain. Put the apples in the compost, return the liquid to the jar.
Re-cover and return to the dark, stirring or gently jiggling the jar, every few days.
After 6-7 weeks the ACV should be ready.
Bottle and start using!

NB
During the fermentation process you will find that in the jar a 'vinegar mother' may form, a gelatinous lumpy cloud, which is perfectly normal. This can be kept to add to your next batch to help speed up the process.

TIPS

General Gardening Tips

· For health and safety ask people to bring their own hand tools if possible!

· Compost where you can! It's a natural cycle and will pay back handsomely with free food for the plants.

· Start small, it's easier to manage in the early stages.

· When planting
   · Don't sow the whole packet at once!
   · Make signs for the plants to educate and add cooking tips too. For just planted seedlings that need to mature, make a sign for that too e.g "Please leave me to grow, ready by August".
   · Make sure to have a water source close-by – carrying water can be hard work.
   · Plant herbs/pollinators if water is an issue as they require much less water than vegetables.
   · Use bio pest control – for example, plant bronze fennel - a wonderful plant in its own right and it attracts the aphid eating ladybirds.

· Connect with other Incredible Edilbe groups and learn from each other.

· Stick mainly to traditional fruit and veg rather than obscure or novelty varieties. A good crop is more likely, and the public are more likely to recognise and harvest them.

Mike Mosey's Human Tips

· Find a base or central location where people can chat and have a cuppa.

· Remember that we all have different abilities and circumstances. We all want to feel proud of what our group achieves, but the prize that we treasure above all is friendship and kindness.

· Appoint someone each year to take charge of seed-buying. This avoids duplication or buying too little.

· Best Tip - Go on learning trips, learning together helps with bonding and galvanizing the group.

> **AMAZINGLY, WITHIN FINDING NEW WAYS TO KEEP GIVING AND SHARING WE ALSO FOUND IT WAS A WAY TO KEEP OURSELVES GOING, IN A KIND OF CYCLIC FORWARD MOTION.**

COMMUNITY

The Incredible Edible model creates a vehicle that allows members to play a change-making role in the community, and in Conwy we have felt this intensely. It has allowed changes to be made that make the group feel proud of where they live and given a real "can do" sense. This is evident whilst looking for suitable places for an edible hedgerow. Mike & Cath Mosey had the idea to place it in a park that backed on to their house. They worked with the local Council to get a strip of land cleared ready for planting and together organised a successful "Hedgerow Planting Event" in the Park for the local community to join.

The meaning of community for the group includes connection through group membership, free produce available for anyone to pick and eat in the town, excess food boxes given to the food banks, and it gives rise to creating events for others to take part in. These have run alongside "Soup Share" events, Big Dig's, Willow weaving and school planting days to name but a few.

Council involvement, such as the two large raised beds provided for the local school so they could grow edibles, has unlocked community resources for community benefit. Community impact has been far flung. One example is Kay Pitt deciding to move to the area due to the kindness she saw as an integral part of Incredible Edible. Soon after moving house she joined the group.

LEARNING

Learning has come from all sorts of directions, including ones that the group never even contemplated. In the beginning we learned from each other, such as identifying edible plants from invasive weeds, and this still goes on to a certain extent. We shared recipes and built on skills in the group – how to weave willow, to be a great composter, and, a very important one, how to be tidy. During lockdown a fluent Welsh speaker in the group stepped in to teach Welsh to other group members on Zoom. 'The teacher' had never taught Welsh before. He found enjoyment in this new skill that he was able to share. Learning trips, pre-COVID, were very big on our calendar, travelling to other Incredible Edible groups to see the different ways they interpret Incredible Edible, forest gardens to learn about other useful plants, foraging walks, and a memorable visit to see a Hedge Witch in Anglesey.

Within schools we have been able to share what we know and the group regularly helps local primary school Ysgol Awel y Mynydd to grow edibles. In this way the group can only look forward again to passing on to the children an enthusiasm and passion for growing. About 1/2km from the school door, and outside our Nursery area, there was no access to a good water supply for the beds until two local residents stepped in. They were more than happy for the school children to use their outside taps and hose pipes. This then tied us, learning and the community, together. The power of community!

LEARNING

Incredible Edible began as a project at the local food festival, The Conwy Feast. To see if it had any traction in the community, it was floated several months before the festival which happens in the month of October. Two to three years after the first event, we stayed closely allied. Nine growing seasons later, guess what? We have our own bank account and constitution so the group could weave its own path. Every October we pay homage to the feast event by having a free produce and activity stall for the festival goers. The group loves to take part. It's a small way to say thank you for the years of nurturing from a local business.

BUSINESS

Our contacts with the business community has led us to staff stalls at other local business events such as the Conwy Seed Fair and the Conwy Honey Fair. By spending money locally in the wonderful selection of high street shops in the town we firmly believe we are supporting them. In turn, some have even given us space to place a collecting pot for the carrier bag charge, which has really helped with yearly running costs.

CONWY TOWN

DUNSTABLE
ENGLAND

WHERE

Dunstable is a market town about thirty miles from London and just east of the Chiltern Hills. It is the third largest town in Bedfordshire and has a history that includes Henry VIII, who formalised his divorce from his first wife, Catherine of Aragon, at Dunstable Priory.

WHO

Sahira Ward is its founder and her inspiration came from Pam Warhurst and Mary Clear who set up Incredible Edible Todmorden and made her think about eating our landscape. In 2012, she came across the organic NO DIG gardening expert, Charles Dowding, and went to visit him at his farm in Somerset, spending the day working with him. On her return home, she organised a sell-out talk from him at the Discovery Centre Luton, after which he visited Sahira's allotment, a car journey from her house. She wondered about Incredible Edible and how that could mean growing vegetables closer to home. In January 2013 she asked the council for permission to cultivate a neglected piece of waste ground at the top of her road. After five months the answer was YES! With land and permission to plant she got organised and hosted a public meeting on Sunday 2nd June 2013 at the local Indian restaurant. The manager, Shamshal Alam, donated £150 and Fay McDade became one of the first volunteers.

WHAT

We have had great success with soft fruits, raspberries, blueberries alongside the usual staples of spinach, potatoes, onions, and herbs.

STORIES

One of our volunteers worked at the local college. The college was having some building work done so we were able to collect eight tons of free topsoil. Our transport consisted of one flat bed, one trailer and a Fiat Doblo. We had to make two trips and on the second it poured with rain! We also had to bag up and transport forty bags of horse manure to the garden.

Come July our grand opening was attended by the mayor and dignitaries. The In Bloom contest loomed and by August we had school kids and even rugby players helping with the preparations.

By September, we were ready for a conference in Todmorden. Visiting the team there is an experience we will never forget! They make you feel so welcome, and they make delicious cakes!

Refreshed, we returned to plant 45 raspberry canes in October and called it Incredible Edible Raspberry Patch, also the name of our first YouTube video.

To our delight 2013 ended with a gift from Bedfordshire County Council - a beautiful hexagonal tree seat - just in time for our Christmas video. We sang Jingle bells and made another YouTube video.

Another year end and another present! A shed! Donated by Amazon! Milehams has allowed us to keep it in their carpark. But soon the shed got vandalised. Sahira had a loud word one night and it stopped. It was then transformed into Santa's Grotto. The community donated decorations and we showed Santa around our garden. And yes, another video on YouTube, Incredible Edible Santa Comes to Dunstable Town...

By July 2015, it was time for another celebration when we won the Cultivation Street 2015 competition hosted by UK celebrity gardener, David Domoney, on the programme Love Your Garden and made a small video available on YouTube, Cultivation Street: The Incredible Edible Dunstable Garden Party 2016.

Sahira says, "You get an amazing sense of pride, and this brings profound happiness which spills over into other people's lives. So many people have told me how wonderful this garden is. Our garden is so beautiful, it encourages people to take a moment to stop and find peace in their busy lives. I've made new friendships with so many people, amazingly kind people who are willing to help and get involved. It really warms the heart to meet them. Without being the founder of Incredible Edible Dunstable I wouldn't have had this honor. Our garden is testament to how a garden made with love can make something truly incredible happen."

TIPS

· Use every means possible to let people know what you are doing...

· Celebrate every triumph, no matter how small.

· Invite everyone to everything.

· Be prepared to burn out and try and make time for yourself.

"WHEN YOU FIND YOUR TEAM AND YOU WORK TOGETHER ON A COMMON GOAL... THERE IS A COMPANIONSHIP THAT WILL NEVER BE BROKEN.

RECIPE FOR A WICKING BED

A Wicking Bed is a raised bed that has a built-in irrigation system. It has a reservoir at the bottom, fed by a perforated pipe which is bedded into 6" of shingle, this is separated from the soil above by capillary matting.

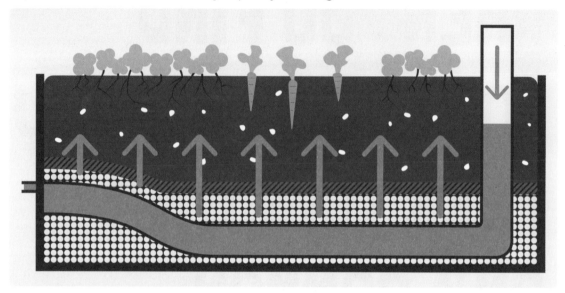

The water from the reservoir is automatically absorbed by the matting and the soil, drawing it upwards. This encourages the plants to develop deeper roots, making them more drought resistant. Additionally, this system lightens the load for the volunteers watering the garden.

COMMUNITY

During the run up to our first birthday, 100 Scouts, Cubs and Beavers from 1st Dunstable Scout Group visited the garden and helped with the tidy up. The mayor came and judged our fancy-dress competition. Red Watch, L&D Radio, face painters, the smoothie bike, and the local Ukulele Band were there with food from our neighbours. By September, we had won the award for Best Community Project in Anglia in Bloom for the Eastern Counties.

In our second year we got serious about more inclusive gardening. We made the sensory garden. Ian, Sahira's husband, installed a water pump powered by solar energy. Sahira contacted the Probation Service and asked for help, and after several community payback sessions, we had a sugar snap pea bed, made from two recycled bicycle wheels.

In April 2016, Incredible Edible Dunstable received the Royal Horticultural Society's (RHS) Support to Garden for Health and Happiness Award of £500 and we launched RHS Britain in Bloom 2016 campaign. Under the banner of Greening Grey Britain for Health and Happiness, volunteers from Incredible Edible Dunstable came together to install seven wicking raised beds in the cobbled area next to the bus stop in Katherine Drive to grow food for the community. The aim was to improve community cohesion, tackle social isolation, promote healthy lifestyles, and increase wellbeing. Our efforts have been successful.

Our original garden was never designed with wheelchair accessibility in mind. With permission from Central Bedfordshire Council, we were able to use a piece of grass verge opposite the garden and started a fund-raising campaign on Facebook, raising over £5,000. The raised beds were made from recycled coffee cups and look like wood. They are maintenance free and will last for 50 years.

We are never short of people who are interested.

A garden will not grow without water. Affinity Water couldn't install a water tap in the garden, but they did donate £1200 so we could install water butts. Opposite the garden we were able to install two under a stairway and to have guttering altered to harvest rainwater. When the water butt in the garden is empty, we have to transfer water across the road which can take 1.5hrs as the pump is only powered by a car battery. As our water is so precious, we needed to save as much as we could, so we built a Keyhole Garden, a water saving concept from Africa.

Ever since we started, on the first Saturday of each month from 1-3pm, we have had Come'n'Grow sessions. These are practical hands on learning sessions for all of us as we exchange information and share skills.

20%

LEARNING

When we won Sustainability Street and received £1000 in National Gift Vouchers, we bought blueberry plants and ericaceous soil locally. Almost all of the money circulated in the local economy. Business people were inspired to help. Andy Godly donated the timber for our blueberry bed. Meanwhile Milehams, The Coop, Bargain Booze, Creations, Loco newsagents, Heritage Funeral Services, and the Curry Garden are all local businesses that have each agreed to maintain a bed. Milehams also donated the signs for each bed, made from number plates. Amazon gave us a shed and Asda put us in their Green Token Competition. When we decided to design a garden with wheelchair users in mind the Co-op hosted a cake sale which raised £386. Probably because we have been going for such a long time, we have been able to tie together the needs of the community with business and with learning. Now that we are more established and there is evidence of Incredible Edible everywhere, I think that this heightened awareness. The cooperation across the community has also strengthened the profile of businesses across Dunstable and this can only continue to grow.

20%

BUSINESS

DUNSTABLE

GARFORTH
ENGLAND

WHERE

Garforth is a historic coal mining town located in the north of England, nine miles east of Leeds and surrounded by land protected from development, known as green belt. The community has a mixture of elderly, life-long residents, and young families who have moved there. It is an attractive place, with a thriving main street, a number of schools and a good balance of chains and independent retailers. Located between the M1 and A1M motorways, and served by two railway stations, transport links are good.

WHO

Garforth Incredible Edible was set up by Dan Robinson in late 2019. It was a perfect time of year because, although nothing grows when it snows, many conversations were had with like minded people. Very quickly a team with varied skills came together: teachers, IT workers, people working in finance, healthcare, landscape design, as well as experienced growers. Garforth In Bloom were extremely supportive in the group getting started, as were the local allotments who provided £100 to get us up and running.

WHAT

The first public edible beds were put in place in March 2020. Since then we have installed beds in many places, One at the main railway station, designed to look like a train, instantly created a talking point. The idea was to support busy commuters with ingredients to pick on their way home. It spun off a separate project on the railways when the operator got in touch and asked if we'd like to provide edible beds at all of the train stations that it manages. This work remains ongoing! During our short time we have successfully grown more than fifty food crops, from roots and legumes, to fruits and herbs.

TIPS

- The first bed is always the hardest.

- Get to know your neighbours. They know more than you may think!

- Talk to other community groups. You are likely to have some shared aims.

- Engage with your councillors. They have local knowledge and may want to help.

- Find your local allotments. There's a wealth of knowledge, lovely friendly people, and lots of spare seedlings there.

- Get to know the volunteers and understand their motivations for helping out.

- Think about maximising your output. For example, peas provide more than a cabbage.

- Remember that teachers do a fantastic job but are often expected to fund resources out of their own pocket. Can you help them with seeds or pots?

- Use cardboard as a weedkiller.

- Consider old decking, pallets or railway sleepers, tyres, guttering or old water butts for planters.

- Incredible Edible is a trusted brand. Use it! It's a huge accelerator to have the logo, font, colours and imagery to bring your story to life.

"A WEED IS SIMPLY SOMETHING GROWING IN THE WRONG PLACE. CAN YOU EAT IT?

YUMMY PUMPKIN GNOCCHI

· 400g pumpkin
· 120g drained ricotta
· 50g finely grated parmesan, plus extra
  to serve
· 1 egg lightly beaten
· 200g plain flour plus extra to dust
· 60g salted butter
· 1 tsp oil
· 20 sage leaves

Steam the pumpkin for 20 minutes, or until soft and tender.

Using a potato masher, mash to a smooth purée. Spread pumpkin purée thinly over a surface or baking tray before patting dry to ensure you remove as much moisture as possible. Then mix together the pumpkin purée, ricotta, grated parmesan, the egg, ¼ tsp salt, and some black pepper. Add the flour and use a wooden spoon to mix to a soft dough taking care not to "overmix".

Turn out the dough onto a floured surface and cut into 4. Roll each piece into a 15cm wide log. Cut the log into 2cm pieces using a floured knife. Gently mark each gnocchi with the back of a floured fork to achieve traditional ridges.

Bring a large pan of salted water to the boil. Tip in half the gnocchi and cook for 1-2 mins, until they rise to the surface. Remove with a slotted spoon and cook the remaining gnocchi.

Heat 15g butter and the oil in a large frying pan. Add half the gnocchi and fry for 2 mins or until starting to brown. Chop and add the sage, fry for 1-2 mins, until the gnocchi are golden all over and the sage is crispy. Repeat with the remaining butter, gnocchi and sage leaves.
Serve with black pepper and parmesan.

STORIES

In March 2020 when Covid hit was when we were gearing up to plant our first bed. At first, the shock of lockdown meant that everything was on hold, but very quickly we realised that something positive would go a long way to support the community. Therefore, the first two beds were installed in quick succession and it truly kickstarted a movement. Planting those two beds was such a simple thing but in doing so, showed a level of determination and resilience that springboarded the project in ways we could never have imagined. In some respects, the project may not have been as successful had it not been for Covid-19. We adapted, plans changed, but still came out the other side in a better position than when we went in.

People and groups we have worked with all form part of the many stories which define Incredible Edible. Some have made little bags of seeds and hung them on a washing line for the community to take away and have a go at growing their own. Others made lots of bunting in Incredible Edible colours to hang around the beds to raise profile and encourage people to take a look at what's growing. All report on their improved wellbeing, a heightened belief in themselves and others, a sense of community and the infectious kindness that Incredible Edible brings. It's not uncommon for parts of the community, who all too often have little to do with each other, to come together over a raised bed. One older gardener reported how a local teen stopped to thank them and commented on how Incredible Edible was a great community project.

The truth is that community projects are usually focused on one thing, whereas Incredible Edible has lots of tentacles that can grow so quickly. Whilst an In Bloom group is the same all over the country, each Incredible Edible group is unique as it has potentially more arms to do other things. If Frances Hodgson Burnett is right in The Secret Garden, and to plant a garden is to believe in tomorrow, then Garforth has that belief in spades.

COMMUNITY

Community is at the heart of everything we do: connecting, enabling and empowering others to do incredible things where they live. This can be supporting other local community groups with knowledge, or offering litter-picking or labour to in-bloom groups, or making the community a brighter place through strategically placed public edible beds or artwork. During Covid-19 lockdown, unable to have big events to bring people together, instead we had a stall on the main street where we gave out free wildflower and vegetable seeds. We also sent out seeds and home growing packs (seed trays, compost, seeds) to those who were shielding and couldn't leave their homes.

Connections have also been made with local care homes to provide intergenerational activities; with plans for the care home to host a growing area and schools visiting to provide an opportunity for the residents to teach the children how to grow their own food. For the adults, a map exists on Incredible Edible Garforth's website to show where wild, edible food grows in the area, whilst plans are afoot to run foraging walks and cooking workshops.

Since Incredible Edible Garforth launched, other communities of Leeds have been inspired to launch their own groups including Kippax, South Milford, Moortown, Headingley, Micklefield, Crossgates, Woodlesford and Oakwood. Time is taken to engage with residents and local leaders to understand what their community needs in order to maximise their local impact. Now we have launched Incredible Edible Leeds as a registered charity to support these and future areas with funding, knowledge and expertise. The project is aligned to Leeds City Council's Best Council Plan, Health & Wellbeing Strategy and Climate Emergency Priorities. Finally, we are directly linked to at least six of the United Nations Sustainable Development Goals.

LEARNING

We work with schools, scouts, sports clubs and other community groups. If our local wildlife group wants to increase biodiversity, then we support them with wildflower seeds. If our local Scouts want to look after an edible bed then we'll create one. If the local rugby club wants to create a community compost heap, then we've got a joiner who can do that. With a range of volunteers with diverse skillsets, we believe we can do anything! We have primary, secondary and higher education teachers who volunteer with us and have been able to create Continuous Professional Development (CPD) packages for schools as well as lesson plans with curriculum-based outcomes. Over the past year, we have supported schools with their growing areas and provided raised beds, compost, seeds and pots. We even facilitated an allotment holder donating fruit trees to kick-start a primary school's orchard.

Garforth Incredible Edible has helped kick-start proper allotment areas in schools. By sharing knowledge and expertise, growers have been able to introduce the children to some different edible foods - including flowers! In turn children have started to see the process of planting, harvesting and eating. Incredible Edible support has helped us in Garforth to gain some RHS awards and achieve our green flag status with Eco-Schools.

35%

LEARNING

We love our local businesses in Garforth whether it's the coffee shop that, as a social enterprise, acts as a hub for the community, or whether it's the refill shop that fundraises for local schools and supports groups such as ours by hosting planters outside his door. Many relationships have been made through conversations that vary from putting the world to rights to a simple chat on what grows well with used coffee grounds.

We've been in touch with other local businesses too, either to discuss small edible beds, more public art such as murals, or simply how we can help them to increase their footfall. When a law firm got in touch asking how they could help, we asked for their wall space. We then worked with a local artist to commission a stunning mural for it that was full of edible flowers that grow in the local area. Local businesses have also helped us with discounts or gifts such as garden centres, or Nell's Urban Greens who grow micro-greens and provide us with nutrient-rich compost.

15%

BUSINESS

Larger chains have a place too. Chains on the main street have been in discussions about community-wide recycling and composting initiatives. All of this has had the aim of supporting business, but also the community, and to increase sustainable initiatives.

Communication is at the centre of it all. When a well-known chain of bakeries told us they'd cleared an area behind their store due to a rodent problem, we didn't realise they'd chopped down a load of apple trees. It turned out, the only ones harvesting the apples were rats! If we'd have known this sooner, we'd have put on a public apple-pressing session. It goes to show the value of a conversation and creating meaningful relationships.

GARFORTH

GREYSTONES
IRELAND

WHERE

Greystones is a coastal town in county Wicklow, Ireland. Once a fishing village, it has grown considerably in recent decades due to its proximity to Dublin. Its beaches and thriving café scene make it an attractive place to live.

WHO

The local Incredible Edible group was set up by parents and teachers in the Greystones Educate Together National School (GETNS), a 470-place primary school. The project is led by a core group of parent volunteers: Yann Seité, Brian Beckett, Sarah Bonaldi, Catherine Dan and Astrid Weidenhammer. Our principal, Helen McClelland, coordinates with the staff and teachers who encourage their students to be involved in the project. In turn, the children promote Incredible Edible to their parents, many of whom then join us too. We also have the full support of our Board of Management and Parents' Association to help us communicate with the entire school community.

WHAT

Our aim is to teach pupils about their surrounding environment and how it relates to the broader climate problems we face. This year we encouraged children to learn about biodiversity by sowing a native wildflower meadow to help protect the habitats of insects and birds. We also showed them how many items can be reused, recycled and up-cycled by building planting boxes from recycled pallets. We are working on making them more aware of the origins of the foods they eat and how year-round availability of fruits and vegetables in the supermarkets has an impact on climate change. They learn the importance of choosing seasonal fruits and vegetables where possible. We want to create a greater sense of community in our school with our garden. We would like to become a model for other school and community groups to follow, to find solutions to suit their space, and to create an environment to grow vegetables and create their own Incredible Edible group.

TIPS

- Be patient, it takes time for your efforts to bear fruit.

- Don't be afraid to get your hands dirty!

- Encourage children and inexperienced gardeners to help with simpler tasks such as weeding, watering, seeding and planting. There's always something to do in a garden.

- Encourage the project group to contribute their knowledge and share suggestions and ideas.

- Create a crop planting calendar to take into account the academic year and the best times for seeding, planting and harvesting.

- Think of solutions for the size and shape and elevation of the space. Even narrow, sloped spaces can be transformed.

- Use the site to your advantage: what is the aspect of the garden – is it sheltered or exposed?

- Consider plants that are best suited to the site and soil, for example, purple broccoli can withstand sudden frosts and spells of dry weather.

- Be mindful that gardens need a lot of time and care even after the heavy lifting is done. Think about drawing up a maintenance roster over the entire year to include watering during prolonged dry spells in summer holidays and protection from frost in the winter. Delicate or trailing plants, for example, should be secured before storms.

- Befriend a robin and learn about the little beasts – children are amazed at the variety of birds and insects in the garden. If your location is rural you might even have some furry visitors. Create a game of spot the bug!

- Consider creating a scrapbook or a handbook to define your project, set goals and gather gardening tips.

STORIES

Our main problem is space. The school campus is shared with two other schools. Space is scarce due to ownership issues. The main area of the garden is an oblong-shaped space that runs alongside the school separated from it by the access road to the three schools. We also use other smaller areas all over the campus, including green areas along the footpath.

Our second challenge has been how to create a strong system of communication between the various participants in the project. Communication comes from our core group of parent volunteers to school staff, the board of management, the teachers, the children and their parents and guardians. So we created a handbook to define the project, set goals and share gardening tips and integrate the Incredible Edible ethos. It was a great way to get everyone to work together towards a common goal and combine all of our strengths and skills.

The 40-page handbook clearly defines our goals and objectives and keeps all of our documents in one place as a reference and resource for the entire school community. The handbook describes different cultivation methods and suggests ways to get children curious and enthusiastic about growing their own crops. The handbook is regularly updated as we gain experience and also leaves a permanent record for those who will manage the project after us.

COLCANNON

(a traditional Irish recipe adapted by Yann Seité from his time as a chef)

Preparation time: 25 minutes
Cooking time: 40 minutes
Serves: 4 people
Difficulty: Medium

Ingredients
· 450g green cabbage or kale
· 450g floury potatoes
· 1 onion
· 2.5g sea salt
· 50g salted Irish butter
· 50ml whole milk
· 50ml double cream
· Salt and freshly ground white pepper
· A pinch of grated nutmeg

Method
Wash and cut off the core of each cabbage leaf and slice finely.
Wash and boil the unpeeled potatoes with sea salt.
Put the sliced leaves into a pot of boiling water and bring back to the boil. Drain and cool them down quickly, drying them well.
When the potatoes are fully cooked, drain them in a sieve. When they have dried, peel them.
Peel and finely chop the onion.
Place the butter, milk, cream and onion in a large pot and cook gently for 10 minutes.
Mash the potatoes.
Add the cabbage to the onion and cook for 5 minutes.
Then add the mashed potatoes, seasoning to taste with salt, pepper and nutmeg.
Fold the cabbage, onion, cream and butter well into the mashed potatoes.
Avoid overworking the mixture lest it become very 'doughy'.

Note: This dish makes a nice accompaniment to poultry dishes or roast lamb. It is also a nice vegetarian dish on its own. Colcannon is a traditional side dish for Halloween in Ireland.

"THE BEST WEEDKILLER IS CALLED ELBOW GREASE.

We plan to use the knowledge of the members of our school community to organise free workshops on topics including gardening, biodiversity at home, cooking, recycling, and sustainability. We want to promote our model to other schools around Ireland.

30%

COMMUNITY

We learn, the pupils learn, and the wider community can learn through Incredible Edible. Motivated teachers and the support of our school principal have meant that we have incorporated the Incredible Edible programme into the school's learning ethos. Topics and achievements have included:

· A secured sensory garden area for outdoor classes to grow vegetables and observe nature.

· Parents, who work in the area of biodiversity, sharing their knowledge of its importance.

· The rehabilitation of a 150m² area of school grounds into a native wildflowers area and insect sanctuary. This (wildflowers) project was part of a two-year whole school programme on biodiversity for which the school was awarded a green flag from An Taísce, Ireland's national environment and heritage trust.

· Planters made from recycled wooden pallets placed on grassy areas alongside footpaths increase our growing space and prevent drivers from parking there. The planters protect the footpath and a cycle path from parked cars and promote road safety for all the school children on the campus while enabling us to offer free vegetables to the community. By increasing green spaces, traffic and pollution are reduced, making the area safer for the children and wildlife, and creating a calmer enviroment for everyone. Subject to approval from the local council we plan to protect other areas from irresponsible car parking by placing around a further forty planters.

· Growing vegetables encourages everyone to eat more healthily and to learn about where their food comes from, how it is produced and the seasonality of fruits and vegetables.

· The Incredible Edible model shows – rather than tells – how communities can contribute ecological solutions to global problems.

60%

LEARNING

Our plans to engage with business are in their infancy. We hope to invite local organic producers to present their work at our workshops and we plan to create a network of local organic producers to promote their work locally.

10%

BUSINESS

GREYSTONES

HARROGATE
ENGLAND

WHERE

Harrogate is famous for its wells that provide mineral rich waters to this spa town where, to this day, public baths are still functioning. In the centre of the town is a protected 200 acre open area of common land known as the stray, complemented by the rural surroundings of North Yorkshire. Coppice Valley is a small primary school in Harrogate, part of the Red Kite Learning Trust. We are extremely fortunate to be surrounded by wonderful school grounds.

WHO

Sam Wright joined the school in 2013 when most of the surrounding areas of the school were undeveloped. It was a great space for children to play and take part in sports but there was huge potential to do more. When Emma Meadus became headteacher she started to envision ways in which the school grounds could provide more for the children and the local community. Together with parents, local charity Horticap, (amazing at providing helpful advice and ideas), and Unity Allotments, (who noticed what was being done and got in touch to help), the growing continues at pace.

WHAT

The front of school was an unused space. The school were working towards their RHS Level 5 Award and part of this was to work with the community. Emma suggested we look at the unused space at the front of school to encourage involvement of the school's families. So we established our garden there, and we made sure it was accessible to everyone at all hours. We could see that not all families in our local area have their own gardens. By sharing our grounds with our neighbours we were doing three things – growing food, nurturing our community relationships, and engaging in life-long learning about growing fruit and vegetables.

STORIES

Deputy Head Dan Cawte wanted the children to be involved in the planning so he gave the brief of transforming the front, paved area of school into an area that the whole school family and local community could enjoy. The children had to think about how the development would promote good mental health as well as add to the environmental aspect of the school. Many different ideas were shared, including a wildflower area, herb garden, orchard and a bare-foot walk. The children discussed the pros and cons of each and then selected aspects that they liked. These were then fed into the final class design.

We now had plans and ideas, but we needed funding and some expert advice. CNG, a business energy supplier, provided the start-up money and also put us in touch with Horticap who had the experience and know-how to help the school turn the barren patio area into a community garden. Horticap support students with learning difficulties and other disabilities. The Coppice Valley children have made new connections through Horticap, enriching their learning. Together both Coppice Valley children and Horticap have brought each other's ideas to life and demonstrated the benefits of communities working together.

Just as our community allotment was up and running, and the school had planned to host an opening event inviting families, the community, and everyone who had helped in getting the project off the ground, Covid struck! Our biggest challenge has been its impact. This has been a blessing and a curse. As our allotment space was starting to take shape the school had to close. During the last year with school closures, we couldn't promote and celebrate the allotment as planned but when the children came back to school and had to stay within class bubbles the community allotment provided a purpose for being outside. The children spent the summer months planting, weeding and creating art for the allotment area. They really enjoyed creating and caring for the allotment. It felt good to have a goal and something we could share with everybody.

Our longer-term plans are to continue to develop the school grounds – provide a picnic area so families can come and enjoy the space, perhaps an area for herbs, a bird hide, and meditation walk.

Often, children learning about the environment and global issues, will suggest new ways we can improve the gardens. Now that our rural area is changing with so many housing developments and less green spaces it's vital we create and preserve local biodiversity. Our Year 4 class recently designed a bee garden. The children's awareness of biodiversity is high, as Isabella in Year 4 pointed out, "We need more bees to help pollinate the plants and flowers which will help us grow food. More bees will come if we have a bee garden with bee friendly flowers" Increasingly we find that through gardening, people find their own sense of the life cycle. As Sophie, another of the children, said, "When we leave, there'll always be a part of us still at Coppice."

"DON'T BE AFRAID TO FAIL.

ROASTED VEGETABLES WITH FETA AND COUS COUS

· 2 beetroot peeled and cut into chunks
· 2 courgettes thickly sliced
· 2 small onions peeled and quartered
· 2 red peppers deseeded and quartered
· 2 parsnips washed and cut into chunks
· 8 cherry tomatoes
· 1 garlic clove peeled and finely chopped
· 4 tbsp olive oil
· Salt and pepper
· 1 tsp paprika (optional)
· ½ tsp cinnamon (optional)
· Feta cheese
· Cous cous or pitta bread to serve.

Prepare and chop the vegetables except for the tomatoes and arrange in the bottom of a roasting tray or dish.

Coat generously with olive oil add salt and pepper, add paprika and (optional) cinnamon.

Bake at 200C/fan 180C/gas 6 for 45-55 minutes turning halfway through.

Add cherry tomatoes to bake for the last 15 minutes.

Remove from oven. Crumble feta cheese over it.

Serve with cous cous or warm pitta bread.

TIPS

· Remember, enthusiasm is contagious. It may start out as an idea but brainstorming with like-minded people helps you to grow your ideas into reality. Teamwork makes the dream work!

· During the first year our courgettes failed, the caterpillars ate the cabbages and we had problems regularly watering our plants. We didn't stop. Growing and nurturing is an experience in itself. We are learning as we go!

· Find groups and support networks in your local area.

· Start small with the potential to expand. We have lots of plans and ideas now we are up and running. Once we started growing, we could see the potential to expand.

· It doesn't matter if you don't know what you're doing! Don't let lack of experience stop you. It's an enjoyable learning curve and websites like Incredible Edible's are a great source of advice and inspiration.

· Find a water source! Make sure you have the ability to water your plot and can find a nearby water source.

The project has resulted in many changes. Sam's role in school has developed into the wellbeing worker. She says,"I use the allotment space a lot with children who need support with their mental health. It's such a calming space and helps children feel relaxed to talk about their worries. The combination of being outside in nature and nurturing plants has such a positive impact on their wellbeing." In general, mental health care is a big part of what we do in school, and our outside areas play a huge part in that. Lily, a class member says, "Being outside makes me feel relaxed and happy. If I'm feeling worried, I can just forget about it." It seems that others have noticed this too since in 2021 the school was awarded the Leeds Carnegie Gold Mental Health Award.

Ultimately the children's enthusiasm about growing has sparked a passion. It's clear that gardening isn't just about the end result but also the process and the enjoyment. The benefits to the children's wellbeing and the development of their curiosity and sense of wonder are easy to see. Our school families have seen it too and been a great help and source of inspiration. Above all, our gardens are a whole community effort.

45% COMMUNITY

Lessons can really come to life when children are given the opportunity to take part in learning, be creative, and develop responsibility for the local environment. Being able to learn outside and enjoy real life experiences linked to the curriculum is special. "We go outside for Art. It's nice to be surrounded by nature," says Poppy, a pupil at Coppice Valley. "I drew a ladybird. I would never have been able to draw that if we had been in the classroom." We have found that there is so much potential for the outdoors to support academic learning, physical development, and emotional wellbeing for the children of the school and the wider community. Coppice Valley's vision is to inspire our families to be "Learners for Life".

45% LEARNING

10% BUSINESS

We are supported by business, not just the local energy provider who helped us at the beginning, but also by smaller firms. For example the Middletons who run a local landscaping business have helped plant an apple tree and fruit bushes. Their son Oliver, who attends Coppice School, raised money for the project last year selling plants from outside his house. How our connections with the business community will develop will be interesting to see.

HARROGATE

INVERNESS
SCOTLAND

WHERE

There is evidence for human settlement and occupation of Inverness from prehistory and it is Scotland's northernmost city. It is the modern de facto capital of the Highlands, while having had a prominent role in the past as being near the sites of two historic defeats – Blàr nam Fèinne against Norway, which took place in the 11th century on the Aird, and the 18th century Battle of Culloden. Today it is cited as the happiest town in Scotland with the nation's highest rated quality of life.

WHO

We are newly established having emerged in the darkest days of Covid lockdown, determined to bring colour and food to peoples' lives. Wendy Price is the present chair, Catrina Attwood our treasurer and Gail Duff our secretary. Most of the seven of us on the committee hadn't even met each other before, but all of us had a passion for growing and it is this that binds us beautifully together.

WHAT

Our very first activity was to plant up Council planters adjacent to the cathedral with herbs and vegetables, with permission from the Council of course. (see 'stories'). Then we approached a medical practice with a large area of ground front and back and they welcomed us with open arms, keen not only to see pollinating plants, but also the potential for patients to join us gardening and gain the wonderful therapeutic benefits of growing food. The practice now has seven fruit trees, blackcurrants, gooseberries and raspberries as well as tyres filled with herbs and strawberries and two deep beds nurturing vegetables. A further medical practice on the outskirts of the city has also had an Incredible makeover with vegetable beds containing kale, mint, peas and lettuce and tyres containing strawberries and rhubarb.

STORIES

Coming to an agreement with the Council over using the cathedral planters was easy. Once we had identified exactly who to contact, no formal agreement was necessary, just email exchanges. We started using three of the six initially but now have all of them planted up.

Using that same Council contact we then created two planters out of pallets close into the city centre on a very busy walkway. This now proudly displays plants donated to us by Inverness Botanical Gardens, and their GROW project, the latter providing volunteer opportunities for people with learning disabilities.

Inverness Foodstuff is an organisation that provides food to share from the Ness Bank Church beside the river. We have just made a great connection with them, utilising a couple of flower beds which the church owns, to grow vegetables which can then be used in the meals provided weekly to those who face day to day challenges. This is so exciting and we have now taken out the spring primulas, and planted a whole variety of vegetables which can be utilised throughout the year by their kitchen.

An area of land beside one of several Tesco supermarkets has long been earmarked for community use and, together with the local community council, we have created an ambitious plan for flower beds, seating and vegetable beds all contained within a barrier of fruit trees and bushes. We have now received planning permission for this and had a wonderful first weekend creating planters and inviting the local community to become involved and share their ideas as to the shape of the garden.

There has been more kindness and generosity than we ever imagined there would during a period of pretty hard times for so many. People have offered their time, plants, seeds, tools, materials, plus financial donations. The donations from the GP surgery at Cairn was something we would never have expected when we started. Words of encouragement have been highly valued.

Our local theatre is also having an Incredible Edible makeover with a large bed being filled with herbs, blueberry bushes and flowers.

Finally, we are planning for the future too as we have purchased apple rootstock and in collaboration with another small nursery, have over 20 wee trees growing for eventual planting in new locations around the city.

We are proud to have achieved so much in just over a year so now we have to keep up momentum and maintenance and build more relationships within the community to really embed Incredible Edible in our beautiful city.

> **IT IS GOOD FOR OUR PATIENTS AND IT IS GOOD FOR OUR PLANET. FOR NOW WE FEEL THAT JUST THE SIGHT OF INCREDIBLE EDIBLE'S INITIAL RAISED BEDS MAKES A START IN DELIVERING THIS IMPORTANT HEALTH MESSAGE.**

OKONOMI YAKI

'ANYTHING GOES'

This is a good recipe to use up whatever is ready to harvest in the garden. The pancakes are packed full of vegetables

· Chop seasonal vegetables such as cabbage, carrot, leek, courgette (grated or very finely sliced)
· Add chopped fresh herbs, eg: mint, parsley, coriander, basil
· 1-2 eggs (depending on quantity)
· 1-2 cups flour (depending on quantity)
· 1 tsp ginger garlic paste
· Salt & pepper

· Combine all the vegetables and herbs and in a large bowl.
· Add the flour, salt and pepper and mix in well.
· Add the beaten eggs and the ginger garlic paste and use your hands to ensure all vegetables are incorporated (the mixture is 80% vegetable). Let sit for 15 mins.
· Heat an oiled pan and spread a layer (5-10mm thick) across the pan. Cover pan and cook on medium/low heat for 5 mins. Flip over and cook the other side for 2-3 mins.
· Serve with sriracha sauce or chilli mayonnaise.

TIPS

· It's good to just get started with a project, no matter how small.

· Kindness is contagious!

· Depend on generosity. The people of Inverness (and beyond!) have been so generous knowing they can offer something to a vibrant and productive community project.

· Homemade signs, setting up a Facebook page, doing a wee socially distanced event for a few hours, making links with established community groups with a similar ethos is good enough and will bring support.

By working with a wide range of local volunteers we are developing inspiring synergies with other organisations in the city as well as providing food to share. We are delighted to be given the opportunity to work with a child development centre at Raigmore hospital. We will supply apple trees for planting later this year and have the potential to be involved in a much larger community garden in due course. We have looked for opportunities where it would be straightforward to improve certain areas of the city. For example we spotted two dead trees that had been previously planted in a recently landscaped area by the River Ness after flood prevention works were carried out. We proposed to the council that we would replace them with apple trees. This was easy and quick for them to agree to as there were already trees in the local plan for this area. We were able to get them planted within a week with the help of a local resident.

50%

COMMUNITY

There hasn't been a single volunteer who hasn't shared an idea or technique that others can copy and who hasn't learnt something from someone else in the team! As concerns about food security grow, we've learnt from interactions with the community that there is low confidence when cooking with traditional, local, seasonal produce such as kale, chard, and swedes. There are opportunities for us to teach skills and raise confidence.

Much of the work around sustainability can seem or is invisible to members of communities; our projects have shown us how motivated people are to contribute to the resilience of their communities in visible, tangible ways.

35%

LEARNING

We have been engaging with the Natural Vegetable Company and Macleod Organics, both local growers who deliver vegetable boxes around Inverness. By posting about them on Facebook we are encouraging people to think about where their food comes from and eat seasonally. This, together with a proposal to create a herb bed for local Velocity Cafe and Bicycle Workshop, plus links with the theatre through our flower and vegetable bed, is the beginning of further joint working within the business community. Creating these dialogues and putting their needs within our own we are already laying down the groundwork for mutual benefit.

15%

BUSINESS

INVERNESS

LAMBETH
ENGLAND

WHERE

Lambeth is a long, thin, densely populated London borough lying south of the River Thames, stretching from Waterloo in the north, to Crystal Palace in the south. It has a population of 325,000, 70% of whom live in flats. The population is diverse, with 30.4% non-White, of which 11.5% are Black African and 9.8% are of Caribbean origin. It has one of the largest diasporas of Portuguese (around 30,000). 63,000 households live on estates managed by the Council and housing associations.

WHO

Incredible Edible Lambeth saw a surge in membership in 2020/21 to around 600 members. All of our group members, of which there are now 125, are added to our online map and may have a page on our website where they can advertise themselves and provide social media links. As membership grows so does our profile across the borough. This in turn provides us with more leverage with the Council. Although many would say that we can do this work without the local authority, we think that working with the Council is imperative if we want to facilitate significant long-lasting changes for our members.

WHAT

We see ourselves as enablers, connectors, collaborators. We don't specifically set up community gardens, but we support people who want to start one themselves. We encourage anyone interested in growing food to join our network; by joining, our combined voice is stronger – and we have evidence that people care about locally produced food. Most housing estates have some land attached to them but historically have been managed for minimum effort, resulting in green deserts. All this is changing, following Lambeth's declaration of both a climate and a biodiversity emergency. The authority has recently brought estate land contracts in-house and is beginning to manage its land differently. The pandemic has highlighted land ownership inequalities and residents are increasingly demanding space to grow food.

STORIES

Despite lockdown restrictions, 2021 has been productive! With funding from the Mayor of London, we have worked across six housing estates, supporting a change in the way that estate land is managed – from barren harshly mown grass to abundant food growing and pollinator-friendly spaces, for residents to enjoy. Each estate project has been resident-led. It takes time but we are witnessing the first shoots of a core group of engaged community gardeners across all the estates.

This year, we have worked with Arup, a multi-disciplinary firm of designers, planners, engineers, consultants and technical specialists. Arup has supported us to develop a digital map for the borough to identify potential food growing spaces. A mixture of Geographic Information System (GIS) and citizen-led mapping has helped us to pin-point the most needed areas for food growing, and the places where there is neglected land that could be transformed. Our next steps are to see how we can connect with landowners and lobby for land to be released to local communities, short or long term.

The Blooming Lambeth Awards is our annual showpiece when we encourage all food growers to nominate themselves or people they know. There are eight categories, ranging from Best Volunteer Gardener to Best Veg Patch. We have a fabulous awards evening each October, where we get together to hand out prizes and celebrate another year of growing.

Money is ALWAYS a challenge! Because we are enablers, it is often very hard to measure our successes. We share knowledge, we provide links and networks of support - we build community cohesion - all things that are hard to quantify for funders who are interested in bums on seats and a solid physical outcome.

LAHNAH'S ITAL RED BEAN SOUP AND SPINNERS

A LONG THIN CARIBBEAN DUMPLING

- 400g dried red beans (or 2 400g cans kidney beans)
- 2 cloves garlic
- 2 spring onions
- 4 sprigs thyme
- 1 small Scotch Bonnet chilli
- ¼ packet coconut cream
- 2 medium potatoes
- 1 sweet potato
- 1 slice yam 1 1/2 inch thick
- 1 slice pumpkin, as much as you like
- 1 large carrot
- 1 slice eddoe
- 1 stock cube

For the spinners
- 50g/1 cup flour
- ¼ cup water

For dried beans, soak overnight, then cook in 1.5 litres of water for 45 minutes.

If using canned beans, boil 1 ½ litres of water and add the beans.

Peel and chop the garlic. Add to the pan together with the chilli, thyme and spring onions.

Reduce heat to simmer.

Peel all the roots and chop into small pieces. Wash and add to the pan. Boil for 10 mins before adding the coconut cream. Add the stock cube and simmer.

Make the spinners by combining the flour and the water.

Taking small pieces roll them into cigar shapes between the palms of your hands and add to the pan.

Simmer another 10 minutes until all the beans and veg are softened and the soup becomes rich.

Serve!

Recipe included with kind permission of Lahnah Johnson, Healing Gardens

TIPS

- Be aware of conflict management and resolution before starting a project. Apart from the considerable stresses of 'learning the hard way', power struggles and dysfunctional organisations swallow up funding.

- Consider reframing ways to meet and communicate with members better than through board meetings. These can be barriers to the work and not stewards of it. A board with a standardised agenda is often dull and may not engage people.

- Seek diverse involvement and a balance between young and old.

- Be patient when working with larger organisations. A council, for example, is similar to a supertanker; it's painfully slow to turn it around. But once it is engaged it has the scope and resources to make big changes.

IT'S WORTH LEARNING THE DIFFERENCE BETWEEN 'IT'S IMPORTANT THAT WE DO IT' AND 'IT'S IMPORTANT THAT IT BE DONE.'

We are encouraging the setting up of community composting sites, emulating a successful project developed by the Brighton & Hove Food Partnership, and are working with Lambeth Council to pilot this. We also promote the community composting online platform MakeSoil.org and now have eight MakeSoil sites in Lambeth.

Every month our newsletter encourages people to lobby for change; we go for zero tolerance of pesticides and herbicides, supported by the Pesticide Action Network UK, and we lobby the Council to mow housing estate land less frequently. We always support more composting!

We signpost individuals to community gardens and highlight the importance of green spaces through the development of a series of walking trails, which unveil the hidden green gems across the borough.

Although the Blooming Lambeth Awards reveal that there are huge numbers of folk from diverse ethnic backgrounds who are growing food – they were 45% of our Blooming Lambeth awards in 2020 – our Board is currently all white and middle class. We are concerned that our views do not sufficiently reflect the views of many of our members and are undertaking a governance review to address this. Many people are not interested in sitting on boards at a leadership level and so we are working out how to include people in a less burdensome way. We have recently supported the creation of our first significant (WhatsApp!) sub-group for people living on estates. This is the first important step to creating non-threatening sub-groups of people who can chat with each other, share ideas, and feed back to the Board.

During the pandemic we have run online 'Lambeth Food Stories', each one with a different theme – from composting, to saving seeds, to discussing land rights, to talking about biodiversity. They have been really well attended so we hope to offer more in this format. We encourage our community to open up to visitors and continue to run both real and virtual garden tours.

Funding received is used to support more food growing across the borough, offering seeds, seedlings and compost. We have also offered 'HOW TO' videos and 'GROW TOGETHER' advisory zoom sessions.

We are working to train young people to act as guides for older people, in collaboration with Black Prince Trust (BPT). The Trust's focus is the skilling up of young people. We want our guided walks to be used for those who would not normally access green spaces, so are also collaborating with the Primary Care Network and LambethAgeUK who are identifying patients who might not otherwise get out into their neighbourhoods.

Our biggest most ambitious project in 2021 was 'Grow Back Greener on our Estates', funded by the Mayor of London (as mentioned previously). We began by undertaking a two month mutual learning process across six housing estates. Everyone exchanged information to co-create a Template of Engagement designed to be used by residents, housing officers, and ground maintenance. We are now talking with double that number of estates as to how some of the ideas thrown up can be implemented.

These six estates then worked to a budget to undertake some 'greening' activities. All the estates had their problems making this a complex and challenging nine months' work. We have needed our very best community engagement skills to bring housing officers, Tenant Resident Associations (TRA), grounds maintenance, and of course residents alongside, to create better spaces for their communities. As a result of learning new ways of working all six projects have been led by the communities themselves.

40%

LEARNING

We know that getting into green spaces (and food growing) is hugely beneficial for our physical and mental wellbeing so we have been developing the concept of social prescribing alongside the NHS. Eventually this may provide a valued service from Incredible Edible Lambeth for the NHS and at the same time bring income to the many gardening projects.

While our primary thrust is not a business one, we do want to enable businesses to flourish in our borough, through the creation of more locally produced food and the knock-on for local food retailers and more farmers markets. We are already talking to our local council about the creation of plant nurseries, a horticultural training programme, and the creation of a community composting scheme. Our breakthrough moment is that Lambeth Council has agreed to pay for a full-time coordinator to help us achieve some of these ambitions.

10%

BUSINESS

LAMBETH

LEICESTER
ENGLAND

WHERE

Famous for being the home of the pork pie, and stilton cheese, food has always played an important role in the county of Leicestershire. Growing, cooking and eating are an essential need for everyone, and can help to maintain a sense of wellbeing in both individuals and communities. It is this principal of using food to bring people together that has spawned a number of activities in and around Leicestershire Partnership (NHS) Trust with the support of Incredible Edible.

WHO

Activities are aimed at people who have existing mental health challenges, and also people looking to bring a sense of wellbeing into their lives as a way of dealing with the stress and strains of living in today's modern world. They are primarily delivered through a small number of volunteers headed by Malcolm Heaven.

WHAT

Therapeutic gardening is nothing new in Leicestershire Hospitals ... as you walk the corridors there are a number of photos taken in the early 1900's of patients and occupational therapists growing and picking vegetables in their kitchen garden. Over 100 years later the concept is back with the "Lets Get Gardening" project transforming a disused and neglected outside space to include a sensory garden, plant nursery and vegetable plot for patients and staff to learn how to grow and care for a wide variety of plants.

TIPS

· Think out of the box, if people can't come to the garden or the kitchen then take the garden or the kitchen to them.

· There are no numbers without stories, and no stories without numbers. Make sure you capture both to truly measure the impact and difference your project makes.

· Those that remain calm in a crisis survive.

· In hospitals focus on small outdoor spaces.

· Maximise reach and impact by engaging, building trust, and creating genuine two way partnerships.

· Choose where to spend your energy, and with it keep your confidence.

INCREDIBLE EDIBLE CAN BE DELIVERED WITH AND TO ANY GROUP. THE FLEXIBILITY OF THE MODEL ENABLES IT TO FLOURISH IN A RANGE OF SETTINGS AND WITH A RANGE OF GROUPS. ALL YOU NEED IS THE VISION TO START.

TOMATO & MASCARPONE SOUP

Forget the canned soup you buy in the supermarket. This is homemade and full of delicious vegetables all of which you can grow yourself. It's easy to adapt to what you have.

· 330g tin chopped tomatoes plus 8 small tomatoes, or use all fresh
· Half a leek or onion
· Medium potato (for thickener)
· 1 tsp garlic
· 1 tsp salt
· 1 tsp sugar
· 1 tsp either dried or chopped Mediterranean herbs of your choice
· 2 tsp tomato purée
· 2 veg stock cubes
· 2 tbsp mascarpone

Method
· Chop leek or onion and potato into small chunks.
· Cut tomatoes in half and place in saucepan.
· Add rest of ingredients apart from mascarpone and top up with 800ml water.
· Bring to the boil and simmer slowly for 20 minutes.
· Use blender to transform into a smooth liquid.
· Add mascarpone and stir until melted into the soup.
· Serve with crusty bread and butter.

STORIES

March 2020 saw three major milestones, an existing project, Knead To Chat, had just baked its 1000th loaf of bread, Let's Get Gardening had it's official launch event planned, and COVID descended upon us. Suddenly everything came to a halt in the most brutal of ways, and we were forced to improvise. We formed bubbles, seeds were planted, and the result was better than we could have ever imagined with people and places creating sunshine and smiles.

One question arose during this time was, "who looks after the people that look after everyone else ?" With that our focus also shifted to staff wellbeing. With physical hugs no longer allowed Hug in A Mug was born. The idea is simple – give staff a break from the pressures of their busy working day by providing delicious freshly made soup. Alongside that, it is a great opportunity to share conversations, smiles and the occasional treat. In some ways, we will never know the true impact of Hug In A Mug but there is no doubt a simple cup of soup boosts energy and morale when it is needed most.

Throughout COVID, Malcolm cooked up a storm making fresh soup for staff twice a week equating to approximately 240 cups of soup each week. Delivered by volunteers, Knead To Chat originally applied for funding from the local council which supported them through activities, events and working with third parties.

Navigating through the politics and processes of the NHS can be difficult. It would be easy to talk about the "obstacles" but we have learned that when there is a clear vision of what we want to achieve, and a clear plan of how you will get there, it's possible to make change happen.

Over the last year we have delivered to a wide range of groups including homeless and asylum seekers, older people, those with drug and alcohol dependency as well as inpatient mental health patients and staff. The discussions that have arisen through running these sessions mean that the sessions can cover a wide range of things including:
· Creating time for self, stress, anxiety, health issues, mental wellbeing and self confidence
· Loneliness, isolation, social networking and activities, use of community and support groups
· Abstinence from drug and alcohol use, disconnection from family and community services
· Food awareness, diets, lifestyle choices and living with long-term health conditions
Determined that this should continue we already had a closed Facebook Group to allow dialogue, Q&A's, photos. Community membership doubled within weeks. Most importantly this online community has shown that its members can support each other at a time when we all need it.

50%

COMMUNITY

We have learned that being outside, getting your hands dirty, learning new skills, then seeing your efforts grow into something beautiful or edible is so rewarding. Importantly these skills can be used at home growing fresh produce in small spaces with patients learning how to make the most of their money, eating more healthily, having an occupational identity and purpose in their daily lives. Collectively the plan was to stretch the activity to that of a community kitchen, and have that run alongside Knead To Chat, (our existing an award winning bread baking initiative), our unique point of difference being that we can bake anywhere with anyone. We have shared our definition of a community kitchen as not being a single physical space but anywhere you can bring people together with food. Through conversation we encourage the sharing of stories, experiences, and challenges, and alongside that we grow, cook, and eat. It's also an opportunity to engage the senses - touch, smell, taste, vision and hearing. It's a fun way to learn and build confidence, and home baked bread is a wonderful gift to share with family, friends, colleagues, neighbours and strangers.

Online tuition via video conferencing was set up and people who had attended workshops were invited to join. It's not quite the same as meeting face to face but a number of them now make regular contributions showing how they have taken the skills they have learnt into their own kitchen.

49%

LEARNING

1%

BUSINESS

The impact our work has on the business community is arguably less than other Incredible Edible groups since most of our work is within hospitals. Even so, despite being difficult to quantify, a healthier and happier patient experience can only improve the economic health of society.

LEICESTER

LES INCROYABLES COMESTIBLES
FRANCE

Les Incroyables Comestibles France (LICF), inspired by a visit to Todmorden in 2012, is an umbrella organisation for all Incredible Edible groups in France. As a result, François Rouillay and Jean-Michel Herbillon, families and friends decided to launch the first exemplars in their respective villages, Colroy-la-Roche and Fréland. They began by taking a group photo in front of their village sign, holding up their tools. This first step gathered support for the project by inspiring local people. The final step was a formal agreement with the local authority to ensure ongoing collaboration. The overall aim was to combine legality with joy and benevolence.

Initiatives in France multiplied everywhere so Jean-Michel and François decided to create LICF to help them establish, perpetuate spin-offs, and interact in accordance with the ethics of the British founders. Adopting the ethical charter of the Incredible Edible movement, they built a website as well as communication channels on social networks where they now provide a multitude of tools allowing hundreds of groups to get started. Pam Warhurst is part of the association's ethics committee and is also its honorary president. The two national organisations enjoy a strong bond.

In 2015, with the release of Cyril Dion's film *Tomorrow*, which featured Todmorden's Incredible Edible initiative, hundreds of new groups were launched across France. LICF decided to recruit a coordinator who responded to the many requests from the media, communities, citizens as well as playing the rôle of facilitator of local groups. Project management, communication, referrals and administrative and financial management also came under this remit. Jean-Michel became the national employee coordinator of LICF and was joined by another employee Julien as technical support for the communication tools. LICF continues to set up projects in collaboration with local groups and give the movement significant visibility, which provides useful local credibility.

Each year, LICF runs "Incredible Days", a big festive weekend of national reunions. These days provide an opportunity for workshops, conferences, exchanges, as well as hosting a general assembly for the entire national community. In summer 2019, after several years of giving 300% to the work, members of the guidance council and its employees felt exhausted. It was decided that the existing team would mentor a new volunteer national coordination team.

A small team, inspired by the testimonies of so many members whose lives had been changed by the Incredible Edible movement, offered to oversee the transition. It was a rocky process. Some staff contracts had to be terminated. Five people agreed to take over the legal responsibility of the association, including three new people, Lydie Tamarelle, Salomé Grasset and Maria Sperring. Lydie, as president of J'aime Le Vert (I Love Green), an urban agriculture association, brought a much-needed skill set to LICF. With the support of Salomé and Maria, she mobilised a new team and breathed new life into the movement.

Since then LICF has recruited Damien Leguérinel and, thanks to him and the others, the team is growing and attracting volunteers to carry out various projects. The atmosphere is one of welcoming new people. Territorial relays for communication, as well as digital tools, are being developed. Ten new board members, full of new energy, have improved governance. A roadmap has been drawn up to show the team's new ambitions. The rôles of board members in achieving these goals are being clarified.

One of the volunteer members, Nathalie Langlet-Gordts, recently became an employee to coordinate the movement and relaunch projects, reflecting the ambitions of the old team and the new roadmap. Subject to the availability of funding, the team hope to move volunteers into paid positions. A new lease of life has therefore been launched for this association which, we hope, will continue to support the network throughout France.

LES INCROYABLES COMESTIBLES

LLANDRINDOD
WALES

WHERE

Llandrindod Wells, known locally as 'Llandod', is situated in Mid Wales in the historic county of Radnorshire, now in Powys. It developed as a spa town in the 1800s and is still characterised by large Victorian buildings, many now converted into homes and businesses. Farming locally consists of sheep farming, beef and large industrial poultry farms. It is the home of 'River Simple" a pioneer business in hydrogen powered fuel cell electric vehicles.

WHO

The group was formed at the end of 2019 and were granted funding to create a vegetable garden of raised beds on a disused tarmac tennis court in the centre of town. The produce is intended to be freely available to the public. Our wider aim is to reduce the carbon footprint of global food production. The first team in Llandrindod were: Dorienne Robinson, Catherine Smedley, Sally & Richard Bramhall, Tony Swinbourne, Flo Greaves, Katja Stevens, Alan Whittaker, Heulyn Greenslade, Ian Scheffner, David Strachan, Carole Taylor, and Dave Burridge.

WHAT

Delays due to COVID meant that the Arlais Community Garden was finally created and planted out in spring 2021. We now have produce to harvest including a variety of peas and beans, courgettes, chard, salad leaves, salsify, carrots, parsnips, tree spinach, potatoes and herbs. Surrounding the vegetable beds are lots more containers of flowering plants for pollinating insects.

STORIES

As a 'Transition' project, the original aim of Incredible Edible Llandrindod was to encourage local food production in and around the town of Llandrindod Wells. We had hoped to begin creating the garden in March 2020 but the arrival of Covid 19 made that impossible. So we diverted our energy into creating a local Facebook group, currently with 326 members, to encourage vegetable growing, sharing tips, swapping plants, and making use of our growing Seed Library. Despite everything, we were able to build an enthusiastic and supportive local group primed to help with the creation and maintenance of the community garden and the development of future projects.

We imported a lot of compost and topsoil to fill our raised beds. And while our crops have grown prolifically we also imported 'weed' seeds. Nettle and dock have been easy to identify but no one spotted the hemlock seedlings until they had grown quite tall. Whilst hemlock is a fairly common hedgerow plant it is definitely in the wrong place in an edible garden, being very toxic! Fortunately it was identified in time. We have put up warning signs and are being very vigilant in weeding out anything we haven't deliberately sown, planted and labelled.

As we began building the beds, a lot of locals stopped by to offer cautionary tales about vandalism. But there has been no destruction or littering and the garden is being widely used and enjoyed by a wide cross section of the community.

TIPS

- Remember that even in difficult circumstances it is still possible to achieve small things.

- Sharing and swapping are key elements in growing a community.

IT HAS BEEN SURPRISING TO DISCOVER THAT JOINING UP THE COMMUNITY DOTS COULD BE SO EFFORTLESS.

VEGAN CHOCOLATE, COURGETTE AND SUMMER FRUIT CAKE

Makes 1 x 23cm sponge cake or 1 x 18cm triple layer sponge cake.

Ingredients
· 250g plain flour
· 350g caster sugar
· 85g cocoa powder
· 2 teaspoons baking powder
· 1 teaspoon bicarbonate of soda
· 300ml almond milk
· 125ml vegetable oil
· 2 teaspoons vanilla extract
· 250g grated courgettes
· Selection of fresh strawberries, raspberries and blueberries/blackberries

Icing
· 75g dairy free butter
· 4 1/2 tablespoons boiling water
· 85g ground almonds
· 375g icing sugar

Method
1. Pre heat oven to 180c / Gas 4
2. Grease two 23cm, or three 18cm cake tins and line bases with parchment
3. In a large bowl sieve together the plain flour, caster sugar, cocoa powder, baking powder and bicarbonate of soda.

4. Add almond milk, vanilla essence and vegetable oil. Mix well. Add grated courgette and mix until well incorporated. Divide between the 2/3 tins.
5. Bake for 25 to 30 minutes until a skewer comes out with no cake mix attached. Cool briefly, 5 mins, then run a knife around the outside of each tin so that the cake comes out easily. Leave to cool completely on a wire rack before proceeding to assemble.
6. Meanwhile prepare the icing by melting the vegan butter in the hot water. Combine the icing sugar and ground almonds then pour in the melted fat and combine thoroughly.

Assemble Cake
1. Place one cake on the plate which it will be served on and cover with a layer of the butter icing. Add sliced fruits around the edge of the cake and add second layer.
2. Repeat process as for 1.
3. Add third layer and finish, or finish at second layer.
4. To finish pipe icing onto top of cake to allow decorative fruit arrangement.

Our efforts have resulted in a group of 'caretakers' who have each taken on the planting out and nurturing of each bed. We are a motley crew of experienced and novice gardeners, local school children, adults with learning difficulties and people who feel that gardening really assists them in managing their mental health.

This is our first project but we have already collaborated with other local groups. The local Wildlife Trust has helped build a large bug hotel and provided seed for a wildlife strip. The community orchard may provide a home for some perennial vegetable beds. The new community hub, The Hive, now houses the Seed Library.

50%

COMMUNITY

There are educational events in the calendar to better inform us, both adults and children, on soil fertility, conserving water, and identifying the plant and insect life that is already present. We also hope it will become a place where people feel comfortable to sit and relax and take it all in.

40%

LEARNING

There is very little local vegetable production here which is something we are seeking to change. We are opening dialogues with local farmers, shops and consumers to develop a supply chain supporting local food security.

10%

BUSINESS

LLANDRINDOD

MARSHLAND

ENGLAND

WHERE

Marshland is an area of the East Riding of Yorkshire, along the banks of the rivers Ouse and Trent, in which several small villages lie. Its nearest principal town is Goole.

WHO

It all started on a freezing cold day in May 2019. It was World Naked Gardening Day but the cold wind in the East Riding of Yorkshire meant we couldn't join in. We set about tidying up a bedraggled looking area outside our local Village Hall. Enough people were keen to start a gardening group, and we agreed with the hall's management committee that we would take an unloved area and turn it into a growing space. We also decided that we'd love the Marshland villages, which run along the south side of the River Ouse, to work together. We love a challenge!

WHAT

We've moved from a group who first cleared land that was offered to us to grow on, only to have it taken away once the hard labour was done, to a group who are unstoppable. We will now grow anything anywhere, from wheel-barrows, to pots, bicycle baskets, grass verges, using abandoned telephone boxes as storage cabins. Through all of this, food growing has morphed into many other things such as food sharing, a lending library of useful things, book exchange, cohesion across six rural villages and creating a hub of citizens despite being geographically strung out where no natural hub exists.

STORIES

We started with £300 from Incredible Edible CIC which went towards insurance and tools. The Year of Green Action gave us £800 to buy soil, compost, seeds, plants, tools and equipment and we started by agreeing to clear a stoney patch for the local village hall. The management committee at the hall liked what we had done so much that they were inspired to take it over themselves, to develop a dementia friendly garden. So we literally lost the plot. But not our enthusiasm. With no land to grow on we began to think creatively.

We put out a couple of sharing wheelbarrows to help people to share seeds, seedlings, plants, pots and produce. We were inundated with offers to host a barrow. We had to bring some really old wheelbarrows out of retirement and give them an incredible makeover. Last year we had a sharing barrow in each of five villages. This year we have an extra two villages involved, which is wonderful. Everything in the barrows is free - take what you need, leave what you can, and enjoy.

We've had so much positive feedback about our barrows, that we applied for funding to make them even more enticing. We received £500 from HEY Smile Foundation's High Fiver grant fund. We used this money to make sure our barrows were topped up with local produce as well as plants, to bring local producers and local people closer together. Over the winter and the third lockdown in England a few more wheelbarrows came out of hibernation. With them we were able to increase sharing fresh produce and food items. In effect they became very local food banks. This really helped residents to access more fresh produce, since many people don't drive and so rely on a sketchy public transport system to get to the nearest town for shops.

As the scale of the global pandemic hit the UK, and shocked us all, we decided to do something positive for our community. Here we were, an already established group who worked well together, so with the support of the local Moorlands charity, and by linking with HEY Smile Foundation's online hub, we acted quickly to coordinate support across our patch in the East Riding.

We started with lots of spare seeds from the cancelled Goole Hobbies Exhibition. We thought residents might have more time to spend in their gardens but not as much to grow. So we cycled around the villages during our daily exercise to share these out. This put a smile on people's faces, which kept us going.

Then we began to think big and applied to Big Lottery Community Fund, Two Ridings Foundation and Goole Fields Innogy Windfarm Community Fund. We need them to support projects that we hoped would help our most vulnerable residents as well as local businesses who were already feeling the force of not being able to trade normally. Within a few weeks we went from managing a few hundred quid, to having around £15,000. Teaming up with The Half Moon Inn, in Reedness, we were able to bring to our most vulnerable residents, often elderly and self-isolating, a free hot meal once a week, cooked and delivered by Andy and Sharon and their brilliant team.

As well as working with the most vulnerable in our community, we wanted to reach out to everyone. After all, we were all feeling the strain of lockdown in different ways. We worked with local crafts folk, Love Wood in Reedness and Carl Morton in Swinefleet, who were unable to work as usual due to virus restrictions. We begged and bought recycled wood, and they made a recycled wooden planter for every household in the Marshland villages- that's around 400 planters. Each and every planter was unique - just like our residents. We ordered hundreds of packets of quick growing vegetable seeds - no mean feat during lockdown when sales of seeds were up 1,000% (although we may have had something to do with this). With our amazing volunteers, we delivered growing boxes to every household. People swapped and shared seeds, and connected over garden walls, across the villages and on social media to share how their boxes were growing.

In January 2020 we started our cookery sessions at Garthorpe Village Hall. Led by a cookery tutor we had bumped into, we made some wonderful chutney, jam, pasta, pasta sauce and bread in our monthly sessions before the first lockdown descended. We also made new friends and connected with people in our community who we'd never met before - this was the really lovely part. Our villages are very rural, with little opportunity to meet up. A lovely group formed at these cookery sessions and we laughed a lot. Did you know laughter decreases stress hormones and increases immune cells, as well as releasing endorphins, which give us a sense of wellbeing? Cookery sessions were part funded by a grant of £500 from Innogy wind farm community fund.

We had a WhatsApp group, for organising lift sharing and sharing information for the cookery sessions. This became a really useful tool during lockdown- as we were unable to run further sessions due to Covid restrictions. It was used in 2020 to share flour (during the great flour shortage), to share items no longer needed. As everyone set about clearing out their garages the demand for this grew, so much that we organised a yard sale across a whole weekend, with five villages taking part. We also started a facebook Swap, Shop and Share page as an outlet for recycling items. This not only saved them from at best underuse, at worse being taken to the tip, but it also saved people from having to buy new. It's led to swaps galore - including some lovely garden equipment, seeds, seedlings, plants, gardening magazines and books, produce and more.

"WE CONTINUE TO BUILD A KIND, CONFIDENT, CONNECTED COMMUNITY.

TIPS

· Get agreements in writing.

· Cherish a good treasurer.

· Remember, even if you don't have any land, there is always something you can grow in.

· Partnerships are key, a lot more is achieved when you work together.

SODA BREAD

Our photo looks like a stock photo but our bread really did look this good!

Ingredients
· 170g/6oz wholemeal flour
· 170g/6oz plain flour, plus extra for dusting
· ½ tsp salt
· ½ tsp bicarbonate of soda
· 290ml/10fl oz buttermilk

Method
Preheat the oven to 200C/180C Fan/ Gas 6.
Tip the flours, salt and bicarbonate of soda into a large bowl and stir. Make a well in the centre and pour in the buttermilk, mixing quickly with a large fork to form a soft dough.
Turn onto a lightly floured surface and knead briefly. Form into two sausage shapes and flatten the dough slightly, then criss cross the sausages over each other, before placing on a lightly floured baking sheet.
Bake for about 30 minutes or until the bread sounds hollow when tapped. Cool on a wire rack.

We worked positively with East Riding of Yorkshire Council's grass verge guru/project manager to identify areas for planting wildflowers following a successful funding bid of £3,400 from Betty's Trees for Life.

We worked with Selby Garden Enterprise to plant bulbs and seeds on previously dull grass verges throughout the Marshland villages. We bought eight thousand daffodil bulbs and shared these out to every household last autumn, and residents loved the impact in Spring 2021. Already residents are taking pride in their verges, planting more bulbs and native wildflowers in previously unloved spots.

In partnership with Groundwork North Yorkshire we helped Swinefleet to continue the excellent work of uncovering graveyard headstones, including that of Reverend Crag Haynes, and creating a reflective space and wildlife haven to respectfully remember those buried here.

We've received donations from Croda and even Sir Bob Murray CBE, although we've got no plans to build the Marshland Stadium of Light!

COMMUNITY 40%

We aimed to start our gardening sessions with our local growing oracle, Dave Hanney, by having a World War II VE Day (Victory in Europe) planter session. We had planters made from recycled wood by Goole's Men in Sheds, and plants from Reedness Plant Centre ready to go. We may be the only Incredible Edible group without a community gardening space, so some gardening sessions took place at a local village hall, some in a local garden and some in the community, planting more bulbs. We have certainly learned to grow in containers, whatever their shape or size. Some of this learning has been part funded by Goole Fields Innogy Windfarm Community Fund

LEARNING 30%

We estimate that by working with The Half Moon Inn more than fifty meals a week were delivered. We are really proud to have helped keep a local business going, as well as deliver more than thousand meals. Lots of people rely on the pub as a social hub, for employment, support for other events and groups, and of course decent beer. When we gathered some feedback from our meal delivery project the majority of the comments were about how the team effort was proof of community. Any obstacles between business and community had melted away.

Not only have we had businesses help us, like the local Co-op donating a thousand compostable bags, and cash from Tesco Bags of Help Covid-19 Communities Fund which we used for extra hand tools, gardening gloves and so on, we have also spent with them. For example we bought hundreds of litres of compost and plants from Reedness plant centre. What comes around goes around.

BUSINESS 30%

MARSHLAND

MUNSTER
FRANCE

WHERE

Munster is one of France's recently adopted Transition Towns. It nestles close to the German border in a valley of the Vosges mountains. It is in part of the area once known as Alsace-Lorraine.

WHO

When the Transition movement was launched in 2012, Les Incroyables Comestibles, Incredible Edible, was one of the very first actions implemented. On the occasion of the first "Citizen Forum", a public presentation of the process took place, moderated by Jean-Michel Herbillon, national coordinator of Incredible Edible in France. In front of the enthusiasm of the participants, the deputy mayor in charge of the environment proposed to symbolically start a first space. With a surplus of plants from a recent seed barter being available, the implementation was instantaneous, and had the approval of the mayor himself, present at the Forum, and a member of Vallée de Munster en Transition.

WHAT

The first bed was planted in front of the town hall where the meeting took place, using space that the municipal authority's contractors, Espaces Verts (Green Space), no longer wanted to have to mow because access was impractical for the machines.

> # "THE ENTHUSIASM OF A FEW ACTIVISTS IS NOT NECESSARILY ENOUGH TO BUILD A SOLID AND LASTING PROJECT: BY GOING QUICKLY, WE RISK NOT GOING FAR.

TIPS

- Communication, education and diplomacy are essential prerequisites. When they do not work, or work poorly, progress is blocked. This is especially important when local authority workers may consider the public space for which they are responsible to be their personal property. Any interference, even peaceful and benevolent, can be experienced as aggression.

- Choose things that will grow. When the material conditions are unfavourable (poor soil, remote watering point, bins that dry very quickly, ...) volunteers can become discouraged, which increases the workload of those who remain and, in turn, makes them crack.

- Rome wasn't built in a day!

STORIES

Unfortunately, this joint initiative of citizens and elected officials left out the local authority workers. The head of Green Space interpreted the initiative as aggressive. As a result, despite great efforts in communication and education, it wasn't possible to obtain the support of the City's services for Incredible Edible. A presentation especially intended for Green Space staff, within their working hours, was boycotted. and the screening of the film *Tomorrow* to all municipal staff, as part of their staff training time, did nothing to correct the negative image of this Transition initiative. Indeed in some quarters it is still perceived today as marginal, useless, even unhealthy.

Due to lack of support from the team of professional municipal gardeners within Green Spaces, especially on practical advice or watering, the achievements gradually withered and the team became discouraged. The twelve beds that the volunteers had made, with the help of the inhabitants, on the Market Square, were removed one after the other for lack of sufficient maintenance.

The spaces created by the residents of the Reception Center for Asylum Seekers (CADA), in front of the Salle des Fêtes, as well as the plantations at the high school, college, and in front of the sports hall, all ended up being abandoned, as volunteers for maintenance and watering were increasingly lacking. But the "Heart Gardens", adjoining the Restaurant du Cœeur", a charity kitchen, and the vegetable beds at the nursery school, known as The Crunch of Life, are holding up, thanks to the perseverance of a handful of diehards.

Having written all of this, some ideas driven by the Incredible Edible reappear indirectly: the municipality regularly incorporates "edibles" into ornamental beds and has recently planted many fruit trees in public spaces. Perhaps some seeds that were thought to be lost will still germinate in the near future?

GALETTES WITH INCREDIBLE VEGETABLES
(LOW IN GLUTEN, VEGAN VERSION POSSIBLE)

Ingredients (for 6 people, 4 or 5 patties per person approximately):
Time: 45 minutes
Difficulty: Easy

· 500g oatmeal
· 1 litre of almond milk
· 2 eggs (optional if vegan)
· 100g of cheese, finely cut or grated (optional if vegan)
· Some vegetables from your plot, such as: puny leeks, twisted carrots, blooming
  chives, dreary parsley...
· Salt, pepper, cinnamon, curry or ras el hanout

Put the oats and almond milk to swell in a bowl two or three hours in advance.
Clean the vegetables, chop them finely, and brown them in the pan
Add them to the oatmeal plus the chopped parsley, salt and spices, as well as the
optional two eggs and cheese.
Mix well.
Adjust seasonings as desired.
Using a tablespoon, form small pancakes in an (oiled) pan (1 tablespoon = 1 pancake)
and brown them on both sides, over medium heat so that they have time to cook
through, without burning. Enjoy with a salad, raw vegetables, sprouted seeds or the
delicious tomato coulis that you put in jars last summer!

80%

COMMUNITY

Our efforts were deeply rooted in the community, all of whom initially took benefit from it. The lack of support from local authority employees ultimately was our undoing.

20%

LEARNING

It was clear that volunteers would have benefited from input and training. Seasoned gardeners often have too much to do in their own garden to make a lasting commitment as volunteers. Without training and support, non-garden volunteers, especially if they are novices, run the risk of become discouraged if they do not have the support of competent people.

0%

BUSINESS

The project did not last long enough to build up mutually beneficial relationships with local businesses.

MUNSTER

NEW MILLS
ENGLAND

WHERE

New Mills is a small town at the edge of the Peak District National Park, in one direction, and Greater Manchester, in the other. Steep hills, an industrial heritage, and a strong sense of community define the place. Incredible Edible New Mills cultivates six separate sites within the town, mostly along the Sett and Goyt river valleys. These are diverse spaces, from planters at the railway station, a plot in a car park, to the spacious grounds of two care homes. What they have in common is that they are spaces that matter to people, but that are a little bit unused, neglected, or simply too big for their owners to handle. We have made them into welcoming spaces where people in the town can work together on growing and harvesting fruit, herbs, and occasionally even vegetables!

WHO

Incredible Edible New Mills started as an initiative by Transition New Mills, and for most of us it grew out of our broader concerns about climate change and environmental issues. Jill Hulme, Craig Pickering, Mo Moulton, Sue Rodrigues and Rick Seccombe as core members of the group, decided to form an independent group in 2020 to expand activities and apply for grant funding to support those activities. Having a core management team has been an important step forward for the group and it enables us to monitor activities and develop our vision for the future.

WHAT

Our favourite crops are potatoes – as they are vigorous, tasty, and fun for even the youngest gardeners to help harvest, currants – as it's easy to take a few strikes and create a currant bush border, and aquilegia.

STORIES

We work in some very public spaces – herb planters at the railway station, a pollinator garden in the local arts centre, and a plot for fruit and vegetables in the Torr Top Car Park. It's great to see folks picking some sage or a few fresh raspberries when passing through the station or the car park. Gardening in these sites generates conversations and community connection with people who happen to be passing by.

Our sites are really varied and have some unique challenges. For example, the plot in the car park had a very thin layer of poor soil over broken concrete. We had a work party to clear old shrubbery from the site and break up the impacted soil. We are currently improving the quality of the soil with soil improvers supplied by local stables as well as green manure – crops such as clover that gather nutrients and improve the structure of the soil. We're looking forward to growing an increased range of food in these built-up beds.

At one of the care homes, on the other hand, we're working in the grounds of a former Victorian villa, complete with a walled kitchen garden now overgrown with brambles and trees! We are slowly transforming these beds, a little at a time, clearing weeds and dreaming of a beautiful community space. A local resident looking for space to grow plants for dye-making, has brought physical strength to the task and provided us all with visual proof of the possibilities. We are also hoping to have support from residents enrolled in the Council's Time Swap scheme.

TIPS

· Appreciate each other's skills: everyone in the group brings something different.

· Ask for support from the wider community. That might be free manure from someone's stable, or more formal funding to support specific outcomes.

SUE'S EASY REDCURRANT JAM RECIPE

There are many recipes on the internet for red current jam, with a wide variety of proportions for fruit to sugar. This one has worked well for me as there is so little I need to remember.

- ½ kg fresh red currants weighed after stalks removed and rinsed in cold water
- ½ kg sugar, preserving sugar is best as it dissolves quickly but granulated will do
- Optional half teaspoon of red chili flakes
- 4 glass jars with lids, washed in warm water and then placed in cool oven (without the lids)

Place currants in heavy base saucepan, the largest you have. Mash them a little and simmer for ten minutes. Slowly add the sugar and once it has dissolved completely bring to bubbling boil. Boil vigorously for at least ten minutes stirring occasionally to prevent sticking. A large teaspoon of butter will prevent a scum forming.

You can use a jam thermometer to check you have reached setting point or the trick with a cold saucer where you check if a spoonful of jam wrinkles when you push against its edge. (I find crossing my fingers much less stressful and increases the excitement when you test the results!) Pour carefully into your jars and pop on the lids ready to store in cool dark place. Longer boiling will lead to a firmer set, and in my case frequently burnt jam. Not enough heat and the jam does not set but you will have a delicious sauce to eat with healthy yogurt or masses of ice cream.

"IF THERE'S AN EMPTY SPACE, PUT A PLANT IN IT! IF YOU HAVE AN IDEA, GO FOR IT.

We want to bring people together through gardening. We've organised two successful annual plant swap events in May 2020 and May 2021, as well as community harvesting days. With our youth worker, we run family gardening sessions at one of our care home sites on Saturday mornings in summer and have ideas for indoor events for youngsters over the winter months. Lots of our gardening is organised more informally, too; someone might mention online, or via a WhatsApp group, that they're heading to a site to do a spot of weeding on a particular day, and soon a small gathering is organised to garden and chat together.

60%

COMMUNITY

We want growing food to be accessible to everyone in New Mills. We've given advice and assistance to two schools to develop their own gardening clubs. Now, thanks to successful applications for local funding, we have a part-time youth worker. This is helping us to engage young people and joins our Family Gardening Club, creating a growing space in what was an empty lawn in the grounds of a local care home.

30%

LEARNING

Educational signs inform local residents and visitors about fruit and vegetable cultivation and invite passers-by to harvest herbs and fruit for themselves. We also share advice and growing knowledge at our events. Our gardens are places to learn and practice, as well as to get inspiration for what you might be able to grow at home.

10%

BUSINESS

We work with local business for our needs, whether bricks for a keyhole garden or posters for the plant swap. As we develop we hope to think more about how what we are doing might support their needs.

NEW MILLS

NORWICH
ENGLAND

George Sava

Louise Maclaren

Rach Anstey-Sanders

WHERE

Edible East is an ambitious project that began in 2021 in the medieval city of Norwich in Norfolk in the East of England. Norfolk is a largely agricultural, rural county with a gently undulating landscape, not flat as playwright Noel Coward suggested(!), and is home to lakes called 'the Broads', with an extensive coastline and nature reserves.

WHO

My name is Jennie Pedley. My background is in health care with the National Health Service and in art projects that explore ideas about human and environmental health. Moving back to Norwich after many years, I found fabulous cultural organisations working with inspiring 'artist educators'. I also found state-of-the-art research institutions on Norwich Research Park working on vital subjects, from climate change to the gut microbiome. I wanted to bring these different groups together, so I started working with the charity, Science, Art, and Writing (SAW) Trust who are based on the research park.

WHAT

Edible East is building a community of artists to create an Art Science Trail to encourage discussion about how we can draw on the latest scientific research to produce food while promoting health in people and the environment. All along the Trail are artworks about the future of food inspired by world-leading science. In unexpected places, tucked away in church alcoves, displayed in the windows of Strangers' Hall and the Museum of Norwich, attached to the gates of the Castle Museum and nestled in the Cathedral Herb Garden, you can find art. Additionally the Art Science Trail ties in with other exhibits such as Dippy, the leaf eating dinosaur, who toured to Norwich Cathedral from the National History Museum in London. Art workshops and a large exhibition followed, siting the future of food in the past for Heritage Open Days (HOD), whose theme this year is Edible England.

Jennie Pedley with public participation

Anne-Marie LeQuesne

"OUR SOCIETY SEPARATES CULTURE AND SCIENCE. HORTICULTURE CAN BE KEY IN BRINGING THEM TOGETHER AGAIN.

Jennie Pedley with public participation

ECO MEAL FOR MICROBES

Gather a bowlful of foraged leaves in season such as chickweed, fat hen and Good King Henry.

Add protein from either edible insect flour made from crickets/meal worm powder, farmed to meet food safety standards, or use sprouted beans and pulses.

Throw in the widest variety of local seasonal veg that you can find such as cabbage, beetroot leaves, grated fresh roots such as beetroot, carrots, onions.

Season to taste with a dash of balsamic vinegar, dried porcini mushrooms (soaked), bouillon powder, soy sauce.

Chop or grate the fresh veg. Add the rest of the ingredients to taste and eat as a raw salad or microwave or steam with a small amount of water till its all cooked up. Eat with uncooked fermented food to replenish the gut microbes that you need. Many Internet recipes for fermented foods like kimchi and sauerkraut abound. Any left over will keep for the following day.

TIPS

• Recognise that food is crucial, in terms of climate change, biodiversity, and human health.

• Take an interest in, connect to, and network with, as wide a variety of people as possible, you never know where it might lead.

• Promote, build on, and support the work of other organisations.

• Consider forming a legal entity such as a Community Interest Company (CIC). Having a legal structure can help with things like fundraising.

Adrian Draigo: Washing Machine Door Dish and salad brunch with... ...and without sauce

Curated by Chris Jackson featuring work by Louize Harries, Fred Hoffman, Sophie Eade, Natasha Day, Keron Beattie and Caroline Hyde-Brown.

STORIES

The idea for the Art Science Trail began when I saw Manipulate's advert for an art trail in empty shop windows. As businesses closed in Norwich I approached the sculptor Chris Jackson who was keen to develop the idea. We talked throughout the autumn of 2020 and approached estate agents with no success. We then branched out to cultural and historic institutions who welcomed us. Norfolk Museum Services, Norwich Historic Churches Trust each came on board with sites for our trail.

At first we worked with horticulturalist Nik Thomson and planned container food gardens as part of the Trail. SAW linked us to the research park and we initially worked closely with one of their institutions, the John Innes Centre (JIC). JIC are working on science relating to healthy plants, people and planet, and agreed to host online talks. Zoom chats with artists, heritage sites and scientists followed, facilitated by Hilary Thomson, James Piercy of JIC, and Jenni Rant of SAW. It was exciting and also tricky since, during lockdown, unable to meet face-to-face, it was difficult to collaborate closely. Initially we had some funding from the research park, but failed on a couple of applications for more and had to give up on the container gardens. SAW then obtained support for the Trail from the People's Postcode Lottery, so we all worked flat out to make it happen. Some funding from Clarion Futures, Norfolk County Council and Norwich Business Improvement District (BID) helped us find a retail unit (we dare not take on more than one retail unit in case we had to pay business rates). We were then offered the use of Norwich Forum, the largest exhibition centre in Norwich for the ten days of HOD. With the offer came some extra funding from Arts Council England for workshops and for an exciting community sculpture from Chris Jackson, inspired by a forest garden.

Many of the artists are about to run workshops exploring food, culture. We have just

Tara Sampy

Tara Sampy

had a medieval procession courtesy of artist Ann-Marie LeQuesne with musicians Pearl in Egg which culminated in my silhouette harvest parade. We are discussing container gardens again, now with Anglia Square shopping centre, where they would make a big impact.

In the autumn there are tours with Norwich Science Festival where we hope that food growers, the general public, and the scientists will get together to discuss some of the big issues that need to be decided for the future of food. One theme is the use of different types of speed crop breeding. James Piercy, communications officer at JIC, said "What people think about plant breeding is up to them, but I want them to discuss it".

The hope is that, as a second strand, the Art Science Trail will build on Incredible Edible's concept of an edible landscape and lead to more interest in community food growing as a way of tackling climate change and biodiversity loss. Again, Nik Thomson is helping us explore regenerative farming, and forest gardening in particular which combines food growing and increasing biodiversity. Gardens can be sites of high quality art and creative activities and places to explore the science of food growing in sustainable ways.

Time is always short. Fundraising is a skill. It has become increasingly competitive in the last year or so. Business expertise has to be learned. We remain dependent on people like my brother who has kindly built the website, Jenni Rant and Sami Stebbings of SAW who have worked tirelessly. I am so grateful that all these partners came on board with Edible East and that, instead of just worrying about climate change, the pandemic, the plight of the most vulnerable, and the future of our children and grandchildren, there is instead somewhere positive to put my energy.

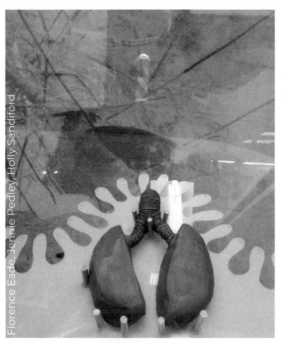

Florence Eade, Jennie Pedley, Holly Sandiford

Curated by Chris Jackson featuring the work of Keron Beattie, Natasha Day and Sophie Eade

Chris Jackson

Chris Jackson

Adrian Draigo

Adrian Draigo

COMMUNITY

On behalf of Edible East I am attending meetings hosted by Norfolk Green Care Network, involving a wide range of partners in developing plans to promote and support domestic and community food growing. This is part of a wider project to enable communities to access their local green spaces and create more places for natural play, mini forests, conservation areas, pocket parks, forest gardens and so on. Partners include Garden Organic, Wells Community Hospital, Master Composters, Norfolk Community Foundation, local housing associations Clarion and Victory Housing. Local library manager Clare Sharland is also keen to see some land next to her library used for a forest garden.

LEARNING

We have learned a lot from people who have inspired the project. My partner, gardener/eco designer Adrian Draigo, treats food as medicine. His decisions for the last twenty years have been made with reference to the effects on the natural world. The co-creator of Edible East, sculptor Chris Jackson, has used his knowledge of heritage and culture to inform the creation of the Trail. The work so far has brought together individuals and institutions from all sectors, linking plant science with archaeological knowledge about health and diet.

Creative activities help to build conversations as was demonstrated by my Arts Council England funded project, Art of the Gut, at Norwich Science Festival in 2019. Here we developed activities for the public to explore the Quadram Institute's studies that link microbes in our intestines with diet and health. Fantastic conversations resulted amongst creative scientists and the public while making the art.

The Papillion Project's school allotments have been working on citizen science with SAW. Their experimentation with nitrogen fixing companion planting, provides a chance to practically test the best ways of growing food.

As we learn to work together, weaving food with science, art, and history, this helps us to consider the future.

We need to take advice from experts, author of Food for Free, Richard Mabey, states that "pockets of land are needed for rewilding and tree planting... we need to triple the land area devoted entirely to natural processes by 2050."

Forest gardening (also known as agroforestry) is a way to try to meet both the needs of humans and of the rest of nature.

The Art Science Trail is expected to increase footfall to the area, using empty retail units to help regenerate the city. Bringing culture and science to people's attention can stimulate the economy and maybe improve awareness of wider issues and choices. Since Norwich has a very low level of social mobility it is heartening to read The Arts Council England reports on the economic benefits of culture.

The focus of the Art Science Trail on the current and future problems of growing healthy food for all in a changing climate contributes to the health of the local economy by establishing the links between food and health. The Trail is founded on recent science about how eating a wide variety of vegetables and whole grains feeds our helpful gut microbes. The Trail also connects us to knowledge of the environmental consequences of current food systems, such as the decrease in soil fertility. Art raises these questions for discussion. Edible East, it's Art Science Trail, and all of the work that stems from it, is a manifestation of what can happen when artists and scientists unite to promote discussion about the role of food in the crisis of human and environmental health. Its core message is, 'lets find solutions together!'

10%

BUSINESS

Rachel Wright

NORWICH

PORTHMADOG
WALES

WHERE

Our version of Incredible Edible nestles into the centre of the small town of Porthmadog. As we are near the Snowdonia National Park, and surrounded by a stunning coastline, visitor numbers to the area expand exponentially during holiday periods.

WHO

The project was founded by Lizzie Wynn and Charissa Buhler in 2016, currently the project manager and a trustee. They were soon joined by trustees Fiona Ruddle, Alison Duncan and Teresa Shirres, along with a small group of dedicated and keen volunteers.

WHAT

Bwyd Bendigedig Port/Incredible Edible Porthmadog, had small beginnings, comprising a few raised beds and some big ideas about sustainability and green infrastructure! It soon expanded, into nearby unloved green spaces, where monoculture grass was occasionally cut by the council. Funding was twice awarded by Wales' Landfill Tax Communities scheme, to support the project in reusing waste materials to create intriguing, diverse and inspiring landscapes.

Our Edible Corridor now spans six adjacent sites over several acres, forming a continuous meandering path of edible delights to explore, an alternative low traffic/traffic free route from the train station to the High Street. Last year we became a charity and built an exciting building with over a thousand eco-bricks (PET bottles filled with waste plastic) and many tonnes of cob/earth mortar.

We now have a community composter, new raised beds, SUDS beds and benches around our main sites, at the primary school and leisure centre. We have planted a Welsh heritage orchard, colourful pollinator gardens and native trees are abundant. All of our sites are open 24-hours and offer level/ramped access.

STORIES

Providing colourful and edible landscapes is generally quite acceptable, but when grass is left looking untidy as we evolve wild flower meadows, or the Council have to negotiate new plants or trees with large mowers, questions are asked. We have maintained a good level of communication about these aspects and people have begun to understand the project and our aims.

Our structures are experimental, part of a PhD study on using waste as a construction material. This has not been an easy process, as our buildings are on public land. We were required to gain approval on planning, risk assessments, and structural integrity, which is unusual for a shed and greenhouse.

Covid has restricted our volunteer numbers, but this has meant that we have developed into a strong and committed team.

We have also had support from the Welsh Assembly. Craig ab Iago, a cabinet member, sent the quote in support of Incredible Edible Porthmadog which appears on the page opposite.

TIPS

· Speak ideas aloud, it's a way to work out what you are going to do and how to do it quickly.

· Aim to develop green spaces around schools, in collaboration with their needs.

· Work as much as possible with children and teachers, to make sustainable choices a normality.

WILD ROSE, DOG-ROSE (ROSA CANINA) JAM

For the months of June and July, the wild rose is in flower. It is a fragrant, five-petalled flower which can be found in Wales in hedges and waste places. A jam can be made from the petals themselves which tastes very similar to Turkish delight. Harvest the petals just before they drop. Mix together sugar, lemon juice, orange juice and water and slowly introduce the petals once the sugar has dissolved. Stir for 30 minutes on a low heat. Let cool. Enjoy a teaspoon of the jam with a bowl of yoghurt.

"THE EDIBLE CORRIDOR IDEA IS TRULY VISIONARY. IT'S BEEN THERE FOR YEARS, BUT IT TOOK A CERTAIN TYPE OF PERSON TO ACTUALLY SEE IT. IT'S A GAME CHANGER – SHOWING US HOW ALL TOWN CENTRES SHOULD BE PLANNED.

Our work in the community has been dynamic and extensive. Amanda Davies has said of her organisation, "Byw'n Iach.cyf are grateful for the work of Incredible Edible and its volunteers. The location of the project at our Glaslyn site helps us to provide additional well being activities for our Exercise Referral Clients whilst at the same time creating an attractive and productive space for all of our customers on arrival at the Centre. We hope that the innovative design can be used as an exemplar for other communities."

40%

COMMUNITY

Our work with schools has been transformational. Comments from Ysgol Eifion Wyn Primary School, under the direction of Rhodri Jones, have confirmed what we ourselves have witnessed. "I've seen the paths and it looks fantastic." Others have remarked on the work, in that it "has been brilliant, and the children really enjoy it. The whole project is great for us as a school" and have also commented on the process, "I'm delighted with the work that's going on, and I'm supportive of the whole idea. I loved seeing children getting their hands dirty the other day!"

50%

LEARNING

We are supported by business neighbours and have received small grants from North Wales Police, Tesco and Grwp Cynefin. We have also received prizes from businesses for competitions we have run. The project attracts new visitors to the area.

10%

BUSINESS

PORTHMADOG

ROBERTSBRIDGE
ENGLAND

WHERE

Robertsbridge and Salehurst are a parish nestled in the stunning county of East Sussex in the South East of England. Salehurst was mentioned in the Doomsday Book 1085. Robertsbridge is now the main business and residential centre of the Parish. The Parish is an Area of Outstanding Natural Beauty with some stunning buildings of great historic and architectural interest.

WHO

The launch of Incredible Edible Robertsbridge has been driven by Helping Hands, a community group with volunteers who perform tasks for villagers who need them, including transport shopping and gardening. Helping Hands is a Community Interest Company (CIC) funded by donations as well as receiving some funding from the Sussex Community Foundation Scheme, with some matched funds from the Parish Council. Keen to bring the community together, they recently launched a local Incredible Edible based scheme with food sustainability and fun at its heart. The idea is to involve the community in planting edible vegetables, herbs and flowers across the village.

WHAT

The focus is on planting across the village. A wide variety of edible vegetables, herbs and flowers are now at different spots around the village. We support environmental strategies, with an emphasis on biodiversity, which, due to its inclusive nature, has really brought the community together. We also planted a mixture of edibles and wildflowers to attract bees. Two of the village children, Elsie and Florence, did wildflower planters which also included wild strawberries and currants.

STORIES

On our first Community Planting day, in horizontal rain, we had a turnout of approximately 30 volunteers of all ages. They cleared and lined planters, moved huge amounts of compost and planted a wide variety of edible vegetables, herbs and flowers and located them at different spots around the village.

Cake was provided made from courgettes and beetroot. The planters were made by villagers, Andy and Neil, who kindly gave their time, and we got donations of wood from local businesses, including Gray Nichols and Feathers. We had compost and topsoil donated by the Bruderhof Darvell community, who pitched up with a lorry, spades and buckets. Plants were donated by villagers and also a local garden centre, Merriments. We had a great time, everyone said it was a lovely community scheme and that it was so nice to meet new people.

We next met to plant more and position planters around the villages. The local doctors' surgery have a planter at their entrance. South Eastern railways have got involved and Ross, the local stationmaster, is taking care of a planter full of tomatoes at the station.

TIPS

- Plan to plant across the area – spread the impact – the more people see the more they become aware.

- Work with other organisations.

- Remember biodiversity when planning.

"OUR INCREDIBLE EDIBLE INITIATIVE HAS SHOWN WHAT GREAT TALENTS ARE ON OFFER IN THE COMMUNITY, FROM BUILDING PLANTERS, GARDENING, DESIGN WORK AND JUST GENERAL ENTHUSIASM.

FRESH FRUIT CAKE

Preheat the oven to 150°C

It's possible to make cake from grated fruit and veg by following this basic formula requiring no blender or beating. Just mix together:

· 4 handfuls of grated beetroot, carrots, apples, courgette, pears, or a combination of them all
· 1 cup of brown sugar
· 1 cup of oil or other solid fat
· Using the same sized cup add the juice and zest of one orange and top it up to full with dairy or plant milk, plus a further, second cup of milk
· 1 heaped tsp salt
· 1 cup raisins
· 2 heaped tsp cinnamon (optional)
· 1 tsp finely grated fresh ginger (optional)
· 3 cups of plain or self-raising flour, if using plain flour add 3tsps baking powder, if using self-raising flour, add 1 tsp of baking powder

The mix should not have an oily gloss to it, if it does, add a bit more flour.

Spoon into 12 muffin cases or a savarin-style cake tin that has a hole at its centre, and bake: 10-15 minutes for the muffins and 60-90 minutes for the cake, or until a knife, when sunk into the cake, comes out clean. Turn out, cool, and for the cake decoration, consider a pile of fresh fruits at the centre.

As a community based scheme with food sustainability and fun at its heart, the scheme provides talking points around the village that revolve around food, where it comes from, and the creation of recipes. The village is looking forward to the harvest and when we will have cooking demos and recipe cards for inspiration. Jo, one of our talented villagers who works for the NHS but is an artist in her spare time, created a beautiful plant map for us...

70%

COMMUNITY

We have established links with our local primary school and already 280 sunflowers seeds have been handed out at a school assembly. The children are encouraged to grow the seeds and then plant them outside the school where they can be seen across the village. Some of their remarks have been lovely, such as wonder that 'It's grown up', and surprise perhaps with, 'It's yellow'. There have been some casualties like, 'It's snapped as it was too tall'. 'Mine is big', contrasted with 'It's still a bit little yet', and more hopeful comments like, 'I put the seed into make it grow bigger'.

20%

LEARNING

Local businesses have been very supportive with both time and materials. It's too early to see exactly how our links with business and the wider community will develop in terms of generating more profile for local traders and food products. Our hope is that our efforts will benefit them as they have benefited us. Certainly the early foundations of mutual rewards are already being built.

10%

BUSINESS

ROBERTSBRIDGE

ROCHDALE
ENGLAND

WHERE

Incredible Edible Toad Lane Allotments (IETLA) sits on Rochdale's world famous street. You might not have heard of it but you'll have heard of the revolution that started on it. Toad Lane is the site where, in 1844, twenty eight working men united to tackle the injustices of life in a newly industrialised town, where shopkeepers would under-weigh ingredients, mix chalk and flour, sand with sugar, and where working people had no rights, no vote, and poor quality of life. These revolutionaries became known as The Rochdale Pioneers. Their first ever successful consumer Coop was about fighting for a better quality of life, good housing, fair employment, all toward a fairer, more equitable society.

WHO

Rochdale Pioneers Museum, run by the Cooperative Heritage Trust (CHT) hosted Incredible Edible Toad Lane Allotments (IETLA) to commemorate their vision. Following a report in The Guardian in 2017, evidencing children and subsequently their parents going hungry in school holidays, the CHT and IETLA galvanised that Pioneering spirit and set out to work with the community once more. Working with parents and the Trussell Trust, they hosted peer to peer cooking classes with parents, hosted monthly family meals at the museum and supported community growing. A once dusty nod to the town's cooperative past became a community hub, sharing food, offering support, learning from one another.

WHAT

Incredible Edible Toad Lane Allotments are housed in raised, small planters on the street outside the museum. This was taken over from the council maintenance team. 2019/ 20 saw a bumper harvest of strawberries, raspberries, courgettes, onions, salad leaves and tomatoes

STORIES

Rochdale's not rich, unemployment is high in the borough, and, like many towns across the country it is not easy for people to find well paid, permanent jobs. But what Rochdale has in buckets is community spirit, ambition and humour, the perfect ingredients for a wealthy food growing scheme.

When the funding for the family meals came to an end, parents worked with the trust to create the Pioneer Pantry, a place where local people could access quality food at an affordable price. Volunteer parents ran the Pantry, shoppers became members, giving them the right to vote on how any profits in the Pantry were spent. Sound familiar?

In 2019 Pantry members voted to start growing food to put in the Pantry. Of course they did, by the end of the 19th century cooperative farms were providing produce for shops across the country, it's a natural cooperative story progression! But here's the difference, the Pantry growers represented all of Rochdale's community from the start, it broke the ground in creating community conversations, it populated Toad Lane once again.

IETLA at the heart of the community mirrored the ambitions of Toad Lane. There's a unique chatter around a IETLA meet up, it's naturally a space where conversations happen between members. I've heard recipes swapped for courgettes in curry and the perfect roasties, empathic murmurs when fears about benefits being overdue are voiced. I've heard laughter as a whole tomato plant is uprooted, and seen cooking methods given a cross cultural twist when it comes to pickling our veg. This can't be achieved in a community cohesion day organised by an external agency. This is real people, communities, taking control, doing it for themselves.

It's with sadness that Covid quelled the ambitions of IETLA. The CHT was forced to close the museum. The hub for growing also went by the wayside, but Rochdale's resilient community will come together again, it's guaranteed. Rochdale has hope, a 'roll up your sleeves and crack on' attitude, in spades. It may take time, it may take some gentle hand holding, but it won't be long until Toad Lane offers a bumper harvest once again. After all, the Pioneers suffered constant knock backs, it didn't stop them revolutionising the way we shop, so a mere pandemic isn't not going to stop Rochdalians growing again is it? It's in the town's people's blood.

- Let people who will benefit, map their own way forward.

- Food brings people together.

- Work with others to get faster and more enduring results.

"TRUST THE SPIRIT OF LOCAL PEOPLE TO DEFINE THE CORRECT PATH.

HOMEMADE BRAMBLE JAM

You will need:
· A big clean tub to pop your bramble fruit in
· An even bigger jam pan
· Jam sugar (we used a Fairtrade brand which was also vastly superior)
· A couple of lemons
· A bit of butter
· A colander
· A wooden spoon
· A tablespoon
· A ladle
· Weighing scales
· A clean plate
· Some greaseproof paper, a pencil & scissors
· A freezer (useful but not totally necessary)
· Lots of sterilised jam jars (we recycled old jam jars, washing them with denture sterilisers first)
Method:

1. Roll back your sleeves, grab your tub and start harvesting your summer fruit. September is a great time of year to do this, blackberries are bountiful and our strawberries had come into their own.
2. Look out for plums too, they add an extra sweetness to the jam
3. Put your plate in the freezer
4. Pop your fruit into the colander and wash under a cold running tap. Try to get rid of as much water as possible.
5. Weigh the fruit on your weighing scales and make a note of the weight
6. Pour the fruit into your jam pan then weigh out exactly the same amount of sugar. So if you've got 1kg of fruit add 1kg of jam sugar. This looks like a heck of a lot of sugar, but trust us, it's worth it!
7. Add the sugar and squeeze in the juice of the lemon. As a rule of thumb we used one lemon per 1kg of fruit.
8. Bring the mixture to boiling point and keep it there for 5-10mins
9. While your fruit is boiling carefully draw round the lid of your jars onto the greaseproof paper and cut out
10. Splodge a spoonful of the mixture onto your freezing cold plate. Leave it for a few minutes. If the mixture doesn't run around the plate it's ready, if not give it another 2 minutes then try again
11. Switch off the hob then use the tablespoon to skim off the scum on the surface. Leave the jam to settle for 15 minutes
12. If you want then stir through a knob of butter, this will remove any last bits of scum, but remember if you do this it stops the jam being vegan!
13. Carefully ladle the jam into your jam jars, just below the top of the jar
14. Pop the greaseproof paper disk on top of the jam, tightly screw on the lid then put it in the fridge
15. Voila, your very own jam. It will keep for up to three months in the fridge but if you're anything like us you'll be lucky if it lasts the week!

For IETLA to flourish once more it's going to take more input from others. Once members are back we will approach external organisations. Could Toad Lane become a site for social prescribing? Could the local housing estate offer IETLA to residents who don't have gardens of their own?

50%

COMMUNITY

Once the crisis of COVID has passed there is the option to bring nearby schools to the site, get kids gritty with mud under their fingernails and grow fiery coop ambition in their bellies.

40%

LEARNING

Covid has proved that the CHT and IETLA can't do this on it's own. In order to succeed we need to step up and take the mantle of the Pioneer's pledge once again. We need to work together to build an even stronger more sustainable community of growers. And once the IETLA growers have met once more they'll know what the site's future will look like, their positive 'go get 'em' attitude and enterprising spirit will drive the rest. It will be interesting to see what business elements emerge.

10%

BUSINESS

Homemade Brambles Jam

ROCHDALE

ROSSENDALE
ENGLAND

WHERE

Rossendale is a district with borough status in Lancashire England holding a number of former mill towns centred in the valley of the River Irwell in the industrial North West. Now famous for producing shoes. Rossendale combines urban development with rural villages- south of Burnley, 15 miles north of Manchester, closer to Bury and Rochdale.

WHO

Incredible Edible Rossendale began in 2010 by a young couple, Joanne and Paul Scott Bates, inspired by the work of our close neighbour Todmorden. We now have several plots in Rawtenstall, Haslingden and Waterfoot, run by a small group of dedicated volunteers for which Chris Adams is the secretary. We correspond with each other using a WhatsApp volunteer page and have just started zoom meetings pledging to help each other when someone requests help. We have a committee of four and have a written constitution.

WHAT

In Rawtenstall and Whitaker Park, we have twenty-plus planters containing common and more unusual herbs, plus fruit bushes, blackcurrant, blueberry, and gooseberry. We grow peas and salads, have a wild life area and picnic tables for social groups. In Haslingden, a nearby town, we have volunteers in an orchard containing mature apple, pear, and cherry trees.

STORIES

Opportunities can be missed when all voices are not heard. This has been our biggest difficulty and now our biggest triumph. It has been important that our local authority now recognise Incredible Edible Rossendale as an asset and have returned to us our right to growing planters in the town square.

Becoming involved with our neighbouring villages brought us new crops and brought them assistance. A small team of volunteers took on pruning and looking after their fruit trees from which we can all harvest. We are hoping to establish regular meetings to expand the group. Together we are involved in trying to create a recently converted community garden.

"MAKE LISTS... LISTS OF THINGS TO DO, LISTS OF THINGS TO HOPE FOR...

ROSEMARY ROASTED CARROTS

· 3 sprigs rosemary plus a few to garnish
· 400 medium carrots, scrubbed, trimmed and halved lengthways
· 3 unpeeled garlic cloves
· 1 Tbl olive oil
· 1 tsp juniper berries (optional)
· 2 tsp maple syrup (or honey)

Preheat the oven to 200°C (fan assisted 180°C), gas 6.
Strip the rosemary needles from the stalks
Put needles, stalks and oil in a roasting pan with the carrots.
Add a generous amount of sea salt and black pepper.
Toss the lot with your hands to ensure the carrots are coated.
Roast 25-35 minutes until lightly golden and tender.
Remove from the oven and add the maple syrup.
Toss to cover and return to the oven for 3-5 minutes.
Take care not to scorch the syrup.
Remove and serve garnished with sprigs of fresh rosemary.

TIPS

· Be ready to promote the benefits of having an active Incredible Edible in your area to the local authority and the wider community.

· Use the Incredible Edible website. It is a great resource.

· Be in contact with your local Incredible Edible groups. We are all different, some of us widely so, but there is still so much we learn from each other.

· Make links with schools, plant nurseries, the local authority – the opportunities for communication are endless and almost always have positive results.

We work across the valley of Rossendale in a number of locations each presenting a different perspective of what Incredible Edible can be. We use the facilities of each location to maximise the exposure and appeal to local residents. Whitaker Park, for example, is a focal and vital part of the community in Rawtenstall. Used by many families and young people for exercise and recreation, by dog walkers plus those making educational visits to the museum, it's a hub for social mixing. We are ideally situated next to a path so wheel chair users have easy access, as do families with young children as they walk by the planters. With this high visibility there are many opportunities to involve the community in what we do.

We are making links with local pre-nursery groups sharing plants and ideas. Additionally, we use every opportunity to engage the interest of children and the wider public. Whenever they pass us as we are working on the beds we provide watering cans and water butts with taps so they can water the plants.

Local businesses provided materials to help us get started. As a result a new group is just starting up in a community centre in Whitewell Bottom, a few miles away. In time we foresee how we will support our local economy by attracting more visitors, and also provide them with locally sourced produce.

70%
COMMUNITY

20%
LEARNING

10%
BUSINESS

ROSSENDALE

RUTHERGLEN

SCOTLAND

WHERE

Rutherglen, dates from 1126 when it received a charter from David I and became a Royal Burgh. During the later years of the Industrial Revolution people visited for leisure, culture, fashion, and markets. The harsh legacy of industrialisation left a wide area contaminated with chromium waste, and a subsequent broken community. The Scottish Index of Multiple Deprivation (SIMD) puts it in 2020 as one of the most deprived areas in Scotland.

WHO

In 2015, Eugenie Aroutcheff and Lynn Semple were talking about how to involve their community, mainly its children, in growing food locally. After many hours and days spent taking children to the park and looking at the surroundings, they felt that they wanted more activities around growing made available. A meeting with their local Council, and the Friends of Overtoun Park led to having a small plot in the park as a trial and, if successful, the promise of more. Although we started as a group in 2015, it was only in 2018 we became a 2 tier SCIO (Scottish charity). This decision gave an opportunity to our community to have their say on the way we were running our charity. Members have a right to vote on all matters within the charity. We also felt that getting charitable status would give us a better chance of securing funding.

WHAT

Beginning with two raised beds made by the local Handy Folks group, some delivered compost, and a few donations of herbs and plants, people started talking. Before long we were growing, sharing, and making plans for more land. Then Covid intervened and the first lockdown meant...

STORIES

...that the group had to become more creative...

Mini-allotments! 150 miniature growing kits, using empty egg boxes gathered through a call out on social media, were filled with a selection of vegetable seeds, pollinator friendly flowers and little compost discs.

During the 3rd lockdown it was decided to provide more growing kits but this time on a bigger scale knowing this would help get the project more support overall. 400 growing kits were made using up-cycled jute coffee bags filled with compost, a bag with seed potatoes plus some pollinator rich flower seeds. It was called 'the potato and pollinator kit'! The idea was simple, but once put into action it became a mammoth task. Volunteers spent weeks working in the cold, wet, weather to assemble over 400 bags, 12 tonnes of compost, 6 x 25 kg bags of seed potatoes, and over a 4000 flower seeds. Favours were needed to store the stock, and more favours to deliver it to more than 400 families.

From these 4000 germinating flower seeds came the group's most successful project to date, more than six kilometres of Bee Line... all because essential pollinating plants were used to create a path linking bees to the community and to little oases of interest. Local biodiversity, which remains at the root of the Rutherglen effort, is at last visible everywhere.

The Bee Line has led more groups to ask to join in and create a longer route to support pollinators, all beginning with those 4000 flower seeds delivered during the pandemic. It has inspired people, just as The Eden Project in Cornwall inspired Rutherglen's Big Lunch and connected Rutherglen to Incredible Edible. Each year the group join in with the annual Big Lunch where communities gather together for a meal with the aim to reduce loneliness and isolation.

Although we have had successes, it's worth mentioning that despite the Scottish

government's Community Empowerment Bill to encourage communities to use vacant land for the good of the community, we had difficulties in obtaining more land. So we made connections with a bowling club situated in the middle of our park. The club is tucked away and, mainly due to vandalism over many years, is closed to the public, with fences to prevent open entry even though it is council land. We noticed that only one bowling green was being used but another three were left disused and unmanaged. We asked the club if we could potentially use them for growing food and they agreed. We went through an asset transfer which took three years, such is the red tape. It seemed at the time an insurmountable task to go through but due to the help of so many professionals donating their skills and time pro bono we succeeded. We are so grateful for their act of kindness and for believing in our vision.

However, we still had to go through planning permission for the proposed development of the land for it to become a community garden for growing food alongside other projects we now want to develop. The planning process itself cost £24k. We would like councils to give more consideration and support to the important work being carried out by community groups in their communities.

We also adopted Rutherglen train station, as we felt this could be a place where we could get food growing for people to take home with them. It was not the best of places due to the wind, but flowers seemed to like it there and, as we were very keen to grow for our insect pollinators, this became an other big focus for us. The station has over 1.2 million commuters per year and itself is not very inviting. The planting was going to play its part in making it more colourful, but more could be done. We contracted two young local artist, Erin Bradley Scott and Chelsea Frew, part of the Cobalt collective group of artists, to create a mural at Rutherglen train station, one that would shout loud "welcome to our place full of lovely stories". The wall was painted and attracted a lot of interest and is still there 3 years later untouched and still welcoming. People gave it its name "Dear auld Ruglen" and we can still hear people talk about it.

Now have just received our first pot of money to finally be able to pay for some of our sessional work, the first time in 6 years!

CARROT AND LENTIL SOUP

2tsp cumin seeds
Pinch of chilli flakes
2 tbsp olive oil
.6kg carrots grated coarsely (other roots optional).
140g split red lentils
1 l hot vegetable stock
Heat a large saucepan and dry-fry the cumin seeds and chilli.
Scoop out half and set aside.
Add the carrots and lentils into the oil then fry and add the stock.
Cook until lentils are swollen.
Sprinkle remaining of cumin seeds on top.
Heart warming after a winter's day out in the garden!

TIPS

- Remember, partnership is key to strong roots. Many connections with local groups help create a more connected and resilient community. We started a green network to link all local organisations called Greening Camglen.

- Avoid duplication of effort. The Rutherglen and Cambuslang area work together to make our community greener, to share skills, tools, funding wherever possible.

- Consider having a hub that is visible so that people can physically see it and connect to it. Even after all this time, with all these partnerships in place, people still did not always know who we are.

> **THE BEE-LINE HAS INSPIRED AND CONNECTED PEOPLE, JUST AS THE EDEN PROJECT IN CORNWALL INSPIRED RUTHERGLEN'S ANNUAL BIG LUNCH AND CONNECTED RUTHERGLEN TO INCREDIBLE EDIBLE.**

COMMUNITY

Our annual Big Lunch is one of our signature highlights. Each year around 200 people attend with various invited artists: the Mairs Family; local young pipers; story-teller Amanda Edmiston. Different activities such as yarn bombing, seed bomb making, a chalk graffiti wall, giant bubble making, all attract people and take us beyond growing, deeper into other parts of the community.

We have used links with artists to great effect as while we were looking for more land we needed to keep the momentum going. With the support of the Tesco Bags of Help, we invited storyteller Amanda Edmiston to do a project to create a sculpture trail in the local park. A series of workshops were delivered in local care homes with children from local schools attending them. Amanda's work was to tease those stories out and create more to inform the sculpture trail. Storytelling workshops generated a large pool of stories, three of which came from the pool of stories gathered by Amanda and which were used alongside the sculptures made by Scottish environmental artist Bob Mulholland, now for the community to enjoy in Overtoun Park. It was soon obvious that people from Rutherglen had a strong sense of pride in their heritage. It felt important to hold on to this "sense of pride" and to give back to the community. Growing food, artistry, old and young, were all connected.

Testament to the depth with which our work has entered the community is the number of people sending us photos and sharing how this made them feel. We are often overwhelmed by lovely stories that in turn have been picked up by the press and national growing magazine. People needed to connect and growing food and flowers was one way to do it, even if a lot of them had never done it before.

LEARNING

We started a gardening club at local Burnside primary school, where we delivered sessions all year round to over 125 children each year, on a voluntary basis. Three years down the line, we got a grant from Food for Thought. We used this to purchase a poly tunnel, raised beds, a pizza oven, tools and seeds for the school. At the end of the year, we were growing everything to make a pizza and show the children how many ingredients it took to make a pizza. We had an event and made over 300 pizzas on that day at the school with the children. You can imagine the success, you can never go wrong with pizza!

All in all eighteen schools have come forward to be part of our project. We feel that this has created an opportunity to build on a multilayer approach to turn our community to a greener, more cohesive town. We are beginning to use this for cycle routes through our Greening Camglen network. Bike town is one of the local social enterprises who promote cycling and are intending using the Bee line as a cycle route. The Bee line is hoping to link people to all the projects happening within our community.

40%

LEARNING

We have great plans for our community garden being used as a hub for social prescribing. This will sit alongside our existing activities where we learn how to grow and cook food and link with food banks. As we increasingly become a place for schools to come and learn how to start their own gardens, soon we will be able to train teachers in simple ways to make gardening accessible for all. We already have a tool library full of items that have been provided by the prison services, and from this hub we hope to further establish a community larder. Adding value to our own produce to sell, such as preserved fruit and vegetables. Delivering workshops on specific themes will also contribute to our revenue. Our small woodland which will be used for local nurseries and children to come and enjoy outdoor learning. This land is a little oasis at the heart of the community waiting to explode as a busy working hive for our local folks to use and we cannot wait to welcome them to it. This is our ultimate aim, to create a local circular economy.

10%

BUSINESS

RUTHERGLEN

SALFORD
ENGLAND

WHERE

Incredible Edible Salford established a Hub at Tindall Street allotments, but the new Hub is in Buile Hill Park in the centre of Salford. The new site was once Bowling Greens. One green still remains, but the other has been transformed with raised beds, and new trees have been planted, with soft fruit, hedges and even a pond.

WHO

'Incredible Edible' in Salford? Isn't that the group Ian started? Yes, Ian Bocock is justifiably famous. He led a visit to Todmorden in 2013 and was inspired to start up a local group the very next day. Ironically the new project centre is managed by a former Chair and co-founder of the original group, Mark Frith.

WHAT

Incredible Edible Salford has established raised beds all over the city, currently maintained by local groups, but if you want to meet the Officers and Committee, there are two regular hang-outs. The Community Growing Group meets alternate Sunday mornings at 10am at Tindall Street allotment site in Patricroft, but the Buile Hill Hub is open Wednesday, Thursday and Saturday from 12-4, and Sundays 9-1pm.
Since this newest Hub is established on an old bowling green, there is a Pavilion available, which serves tea and biscuits (thanks to The Friends of Buile Hill Park) and provides the only accessible toilet in the whole 120 acres! (You can also join in croquet on Thursday and Saturday afternoons.)

STORIES

Incredible Edible Salford was lucky to have a founder member with a vision, and the energy to make things happen, both in Salford and across the Incredible Edible Network. Ian Bocock has moved on now, but only to better things – his new Community Interest Company (CIC) called 'Incredible Education'. Luckily, a co-founder and ex-Chair, Mark Frith, has taken up the reins, with a new vision, at a new 5 acre site. The ethics and purpose for Incredible Edibles in Salford is as strong as ever. It's no coincidence that Incredible Edible Salford's Secretary, Mike Scantlebury, is the author of the Incredible Edible anthem, a song that is spreading across iTunes, Spotify, SoundCloud and YouTube, and sung by The Jane and Mike Band. As the chorus says,

'It's Incredible, it's Edible, it's invaluable to me.
It's Incredible, you can eat it all, and best of all, it's free.
Plant gardens or containers, raised beds or a bin,
And don't forget the motto - If you eat, you're in.'

DAILY TEA

Every morning I make up the teapots for the day.

One is stimulating. Achieve this by using easy-grow mint picked fresh.

One is calming. This has a mixture of lemon balm and barley. Add nettles or dandelions, if they are in season. They are best when young and tender. They may be cooked as a base for a soup the following day. Self-pick herbal teas make the most of your time and minimise cooking and preparation time. Also, you can live healthily and cheaply.

Barley can be easily grown in this country, which means minimal food miles but like rice needs to be cooked and can't be eaten raw. Soaking it in the teapot cuts down on cooking time. It is a grain that stabilises blood sugar and maintains energy levels. It also contains magnesium which is a common deficiency in a lot of diets.

"If you eat easy mint, you will never be skint and it gives you get up and go.
If you eat lemon balm it keeps you calm from your head down to your toe."
(teas and ditto both courtesy of Jane Wood)

TIPS

- Make sure the Chair of your project is the one with the most horticultural knowledge, because that's the person that all the members are going to turn to, when they don't recognise a plant, or wonder why a leaf is turning brown.

- Don't divide visitors into Workers or Supporters. They can be both. When Salford's elected Mayor visited us recently, he picked up a spade!

- Don't ignore the neighbours! No matter where your site, you're going to need the approval of the people in the nearest houses.

- Don't be funny about money. It's always useful. Don't turn donations down.

"PROVIDING TEA AND BISCUITS AND AN ACCESSIBLE TOILET? ESSENTIAL!

Incredible Edible Salford shares our new site with The Friends of Buile Hill Park, who represent all sorts of local people, and support running, cycling, health walks, croquet, pram pushing and dog walking in the park. We are very aware we are part of the wider community and the houses nearby, but believe our message of 'Green and Growing' is for everyone.

40%

COMMUNITY

Our new site has 30 small plots available to local people to grow what they want, the way they want it. Along the sides are half a dozen larger Incredible Edible plots, managed by a team of volunteers. This means that help and advice is always on hand. Also, our key people have teaching and counselling qualifications, and hope to offer social prescribing in future. We see Incredible Edible Salford as being all about therapeutic horticulture. Many people came to the site during the Covid lockdown looking for companionship, fresh air and a green environment. We want to help everyone make the most of this.

40%

LEARNING

'Business' is everywhere. We hope to run Incredible Edible Salford in a business-like manner, and are keen to report to our members and funders on a regular basis. We have already spawned one new business, 'Incredible Education', and another CIC is being registered at the moment - 'Growing Togetherness'. We have recently received input from Salford University Business School, and are talking to local businesses about long-term financial and volunteer inputs. We are always grateful to receive soil, chippings, straw and pallets from local businesses. Thanks also to Salford City Council who keep the lawns cut and - so far - haven't charged for electricity and water. A useful donation!

20%

BUSINESS

SALFORD

SAN ISIDRO
ARGENTINA

WHERE

San Isidro is 20 kilometers north of the city of Buenos Aires. On its eastern border is the Río de La Plata and its nature reserve. Immediately next to it there used to be a wide green sidewalk filled with piles of rubble. This is where we set up our first vegetable box and composting bin and Huertavereda La Ribera was born.

WHO

During the 2020 Covid lockdown, a group of neighbours in our mid thirties started working the soil of public spaces. Most of us didn't know each other, but we all wanted to give back to the earth, to address all the damage we've been doing. We were all sure that this was the way. We thought, 'Let's try' and all of us, Marcos, Batata, Sofi P., Maria, Urraca, Mati, Juampi, Cami, Matute, Juanma, Feli, Lucas, Toti, Julie and Sofi G., without any funding or external organisation, became friends and colleagues in this effort. Special thanks to Cheli Di Paolo for the photos.

WHAT

August 1st, which is Pachamama, or Mother Earth's Day, we set our first composting bin. The soil we had chosen was very damaged and our commitment was to recover it with the neighbours' organic waste. This was the perfect excuse to incentivise more people to get to know the project and the sustainable cycle of composting. We made the raised beds from discarded pallets we found in the streets and we gave them a coat or two of burnt car oil for protection. The reusing of materials has always been our priority. We filled the boxes with earth recovered from constructions, river soil, horse manure and our wonderful compost. Neighbours brought seedlings of their own production, eager to see them grow. We set up benches, tables, a bicycle rack and a mailbox where passers-by can leave their seeds.

TIPS

· Write informative and motivating messages on wooden boxes.

· Have a blackboard or a space to make announcements, ask for things, etc.

· Set at least 1 fixed day per week to work and encourage new people to join.

· Open your mind to new learning, new activities, new experiences with people. This is the beginning of a strong community.

· Keep it tidy.

· Keep in touch with other green gardens in the area to share experiences.

· Better to forgive than to ask for permission, but do have good relations with local authorities, invite them to see your work and to notice all the benefits provided to the community. This will promote expansion.

"IT IS MUCH EASIER TO APOLOGISE FOR IMPLEMENTING A GOOD IDEA THAN IT IS TO GET PERMISSION.

SRI RACHA & EMPANADA

Combine these two for a perfect meal.

The sauce: Sri Racha Ribereña
Sauté in scant olive oil, 1 onion, 1 green pepper, 2 cloves of garlic, 2 small tomatoes, 3 red chillies, mixed herbs over medium heat. Blend until smooth, and season to taste with wine vinegar, salt, pepper and a dash of olive oil.

The empanada: Borage, Pumpkin & Ricotta
Use home-made or bought pastry – puff or shortcrust. Roll it out and cut circles that will then be folded over to form pasties. Brush water or egg around the edges as 'glue' and stuff with a filling made from: the puréed pulp of 1 roasted and de-seeded pumpkin, added to a sautéed medley of 3 garlic cloves, 1 sliced leek and 1 chopped onion, borage or star flower with mixed herbs and salt to taste. Before folding the pasties closed, add a spoonful or ricotta or vegan alternative. Fold the pasty and bake until golden brown.
PS: Save the seeds of all the ingredients!

STORIES

From the beginning we knew we wanted a space open 24/7 for everyone. The idea of planting in boxes was to avoid dogs or people walking on top of the vegetable beds. We realized that this was also an opportunity for people with mobility issues to work the soil. Without planning much, we ended up having twenty-six vegetable boxes, so we started making terraces in the rubble piles that were left. We improved the soil and made fourteen terraces for more vegetables.

A neighbouring sailing club, Club Náutico Las Barrancas, provided water and we set up a watering calendar to make sure all the plants got water, especially during summer.

None of this could have been achieved without the support of people within the authorities involved in our area. People like Leandro Martin (Director of Public Spaces in San Isidro), and Gabi Martinez (local councillor). Others like Fran Ottonello, Victor, Martin Mom from Rehau Argentina, Vivero del Puerto, Hipico de San Isidro, Ceamse, Coco de Correcaminos and especially all the neighbours of El Bajo de San Isidro.

The inspiration to unite us all was very much the TED talk from Pam Warhurst and Incredible Edible.

A couple of blocks away from where we put our first raised bed, there's a humble neighbourhood with a semi abandoned garden. Our new project, and the motivation of neighbours, kickstarted its recovery. It was also the perfect opportunity to initiate activities with children from the neighbourhood. The economic frontiers that divided both areas started to disappear. Today we all greet each other by our names thanks to the dialogue that was generated due to planting vegetables in public spaces.

We also found that to complete this sustainable cycle, we needed to generate an ecological hub that involved more people from the community. With recovered pallets we built three containers for neighbours to dispose of their clean and dry recyclables. A cooperative society committed to picking up the recyclables every week. Today, neighbours come to Huertavereda La Ribera with their organic waste to be composted, and also their recyclables for the containers, contributing to a huge reduction of garbage taken to landfills.

50% COMMUNITY

We had to learn everything from the beginning, we went back to being children and being dazzled by the first butterflies that came to the milkweeds, the aubergines and their flowers, the mustard leaves. We learned to improve the soil that had been injured by human mistreatment. We learned that this space is much more than a garden. It is a community sustained thanks to the commitment of the neighbours that began it and those who joined. Through our learning others have also learned and replicated the project elsewhere.

40% LEARNING

As lockdown restrictions started to ease, we began to meet more people interested in the project and eager to promote it.
· A lady that organises walking tours included us in her circuit.
· Children's workshops choose the space to do outdoor learning activities and games.
· Bocas Abiertas, a local food festival added all community green gardens of the area as must stops of the restaurants tour.
· Huertavereda became an obligatory visit to anyone coming to San Isidro.
· All of this generates income and strengthens a local circular economy that benefits everyone.
The space that a year ago was an abandoned lot, is today a park taken care of by its neighbours. We learned that having a safe public space depends entirely on who uses it and takes care of it. We dreamt of an edible neighbourhood and we believe that the best way of making dreams come true is by simply doing it.

10% BUSINESS

SAN ISIDRO

SOUTH ORMSBY

ENGLAND

WHERE

Our quietly active village of South Ormsby is nestled in the heart of the Lincolnshire Wolds. It's positioned in a roughly central area eight miles from the town of Louth, ten miles from Horncastle and sixteen miles from the iconic seaside attractions of Skegness. Characterised by rolling hills, woods, and chalk streams, few places symbolise the English countryside more perfectly.

WHO

From the spring of 2021 a diverse group of people have come together and developed into our Incredible Edible network. We grew from just a few people raising a rabbit-proof fence, to a group of over 15 people both from the local area, and visitors from elsewhere in the county, all meeting up to make new friends and build a garden together with Jacqui Rhodes, Jack Waters, Viki Shores, Sam Shores and Pete Coxon.

WHAT

Fuelled by regular afternoon coffees and long sessions at the local pub, we have used an organic 'no dig' growing method in which we seek to disturb the natural soil cycles as little as possible and use only organic manures, composts and fertilisers. While largely trial and error, our eco-friendly efforts have paid off in dividends of strawberries, runner beans, rainbow chard and much more! Going forward, we plan to continue the success of our garden with monthly barbecues into the summer and further regular meet-ups in between and beyond, whilst feeding the community lots of healthy produce.

STORIES

During our 'Have A Grow Day' event in early June 2021, families, friends and kids built garden furniture out of donated pallets (definitely safe!) and dug out long-forgotten seed packets from their sheds for a sunny day of planting and muddy fingers. We also built several bike racks out of the same recycled pallets, which turned out to be surprisingly sturdy and practical!

The year's growing season began slowly with the late frosts in April, which put the brakes on our seedlings and much of the early planting. While the summer months have been fairly kind, with rain and sun in dual measure, any sustained sunshine beats down hard on the shallow, cardboard-lined no-dig plots in which our vegetables grow. Water has been a real issue, but our dedicated volunteers have kept everything ticking over brilliantly. The team spent regular hours watering the vegetable beds which solved any issues with dry weather for much of the garden's young life, and now we are in the process of organising a solar-powered water pump to sustainably solve these issues for the long term.

"COMMUNITY GARDENS" ARE MADE FROM BOTH A GARDEN AND THE PEOPLE THAT IT BRINGS TOGETHER. WE FIND THE LATTER TO BE THE TRUE IMPORTANCE.

FRESH STRAWBERRIES & HOMEMADE MERINGUE

'Fresh strawberries taste the best in the most simple of recipes' – Jacqui Rhodes

You will need:
· 4 eggs (whites)
· 8oz caster sugar
· Fresh cream
· Strawberries

Separate the egg whites. Discard the yolks for later use.
Whisk the whites in a clean bowl until stiff and look like clouds.
At medium speed add the sugar 1 tbl at a time – whisk until stiff and shiny.
Pipe, spoon or spread the meringue as preferred
Bake in preheated oven at 120°C for 1-1.5 hours.

When cooled:
Whip the cream, centre it on the meringue, and add fresh strawberries as desired.

Decoration (optional): Strawberry Sauce
· Puree 8oz strawberries in a blender
· Push through a sieve, discarding the seeds
· Stir in 2 tsps icing sugar and a squeeze of lemon
· Refrigerate until ready to serve
· Drizzle over the desert and add a sprig of mint to finish it off!

TIPS

All of our tips are about watering!
· 'Water, water, water' is South Ormsby Estate's resident veteran gardener's top tip. Simple, yet essential in our case, many times it has elicited several chuckles.

· Water regularly if topsoil is scarce and/ or drainage is high due to sloped land or sandy soil (all of which are the case for us). Aside from lots of naturally sourced mulch such as woodchips or compost, watering is the best thing to do.

· Ants love dry soil. Many plants detest erratic moisture levels, leaving them weaker to infection and stunted in their growth. Water!

· Make sure your manure is well-rotted before mixing it into soil, or else it will burn your plants' roots and be unsuitable for growing.

Incredible Edible South Ormsby is wholly driven by the community through constant social media interaction and organisation. We hold weekly official meet-ups over hot drinks and most evenings after work people drift over to the veg plot to follow sound advice and keep everything hydrated.

COMMUNITY

We encourage everyone to get involved in some capacity, no matter their knowledge level. Whether it's as simple as knowing how to pull out a weed for good, or picking out a plot and planting one's own seeds for fun, all are welcome. We recommend several gardening books to all our volunteers, some from well-known sources such as the Royal Horticultural Society, and some from little-known, small authors who wrote down their old-timer tips and tricks for future generations.

LEARNING

Any business aspect will likely never be a large priority for us, but we have a few things on the near horizon. We plan to set up a small stand with an honesty box by our plot this summer, offering our produce to the local village and passing walkers.

BUSINESS

SOUTH ORMSBY

SOUTHALL
ENGLAND

WHERE

Up until the 19th century Southall was a rural village surrounded by farmland. Now it is just a few miles from Heathrow, Europe's busiest airport. As London expanded over the years, it became increasingly industrialised and populated. Southall now hosts a diverse population with one of the largest Asian communities in London, and among the highest concentrations of people from the Sikh faith outside of India. Colloquially known as 'Little Punjab' or 'Little India', many 1950s immigrants came from rural backgrounds steeped in agriculture and slowly moved away from their agricultural roots. This is a trend that some of today's inhabitants of Southall are seeking to reverse.

WHO

In 2014 a few locals got together to help Southall join the growing Transition Town movement founded by Rob Hopkins in Totnes in 2007. March 2015 saw the official launch of Southall Transition. Its mission was to respond to climate change, peak oil prices, and economic instability by encouraging 'local people to take responsibility through practical action' with a view to 'building resilient communities'. The Southall organisation is 100% volunteer run and currently has just over 400 members. Mani Dhanda was one of its founding members, initially acting as project manager and taking the lead on all projects delivered by the organisation. In 2019 he became its chair.

WHAT

Food security was the main concern of the residents surveyed, so planting fruit/ nut trees for foraging proved popular. The goal in 2015 was to plant five orchards, in five publicly accessible spaces within five years. The Southall Orchard Project (SOP) was successfully completed in 2020 resulting in over 200 more fruit/ nut trees and thousands of fruiting hedges planted throughout the town. In 2016, a year into the SOP, Mani came across Incredible Edible. In January 2017 Pam Warhurst attended as the key note speaker and generated great enthusiasm. By October 2017, the town's first roadside edible 'garden' was opened outside West London College.

STORIES

Pam's appearance at Southall's Dominion Centre was co-hosted with Ealing Transition and went on to spur further collaboration with numerous groups and organisations. This capacity to join with others when and wherever needed has been a common theme with other Incredible Edible groups we have learned about. The entire idea of sharing has also led us to the sorts of agreements where Southall Transition agrees to maintain beds for the first year and thereafter pass the responsibility to others.

Following talks with the local authority in 2019, permission was granted to build raised beds onto the public highway at two locations in the town. In 2020 the COVID-19 pandemic took hold and the lock down restrictions made it difficult to proceed. Nevertheless, much of the year was spent seeking funds for another Incredible Edible bed. Towards the end of 2020, Southall Transition had managed to secure the necessary funding from The Transition Network Bounce Forward scheme funded by the National Lottery Community Fund. Further assistance was granted by Southall Lions Club and Ealing Council. Consequently work commenced on Southall's second Incredible Edible bed outside Greenfields Nursery School and Children's Centre in early 2021, resulting in its completion by April 2021. Once again Southall Transition agreed to maintain the bed for the first 12 months before handing responsibility over to the nursery.

We shamelessly use the opening of any new site as an opportunity to invite local dignitaries. No matter how small the bed or how few plants they have, there is an occasion to be marked. Community

growing is non-partisan and politicians are generally happy to show up and help us promote the work.

In addition to aiming to achieve the objectives of Incredible Edible, two further factors are considered in the design of beds. Firstly we consider ease of maintenance. Our beds are planted mostly with perennial edibles to ensure that they can be easily cared for, requiring just 1-2 hours of labour each month, with weeding being the main task if no further changes are desired. Secondly, under Mani's guidance, we subscribe to the 'broken windows' theory, designing beds that are pleasing to the eye and can brighten up the general area with a view to discouraging vandalism and litter.

We think we have achieved these aims and often receive positive comments from passersby during the construction phases.

We have, however, had our challenges. During the implementation of phase 4 of the Southall Orchard Project, metal cages were introduced as a counter vandalism measure following attacks on trees at some of the earlier orchards. Although these pushed up the cost of the project substantially they have proved fairly successful at deterring further vandalism and as a bonus they also look quite good.

We are lucky to have the Local Authority Highways Department permission still in place for another raised bed on the public highway. Mani believes the town's fire station would make an excellent flagship site.

"HOWEVER SMALL OUR TRIUMPHS, WE BROADCAST THEM WIDELY.

CURRIED VEGETABLES

The key to a good fresh vegetable curry is:
· first, the base 'holy trinity' of 1 part fresh grated garlic and 1 part fresh grated ginger and 2 parts diced onion with a curry blend of your choice, and
· second, never adding water. For 2 people, using 1 tablespoon as your measure, sauté the holy trinity and spices to your taste in 2 tablespoons of light cooking oil. When it is cooked, not crisp, add 4 handfuls of chopped seasonal vegetables. Cover and cook slowly until the vegetables are tender. The fluids from inside the vegetables do all the work. Salt to taste and serve with bread, potatoes, or rice.

TIPS

· Make clear arrangements for care of beds to pass over to others. For example, with the schools, you do it for the first year, then it's over to them.

· Celebrate every triumph, however small, with an event - inviting local worthies and dignitaries - they love it and it gives profile to the project.

· Be prepared to have to do it all yourself when you start.

· Beware the many departments within the local authority that you may need to work with: housing, planning, highways etc. and don't let yourself be downcast.

· Be clear about what you need.

· Getting volunteers is great, but they need to be the 'right' volunteers.

We have a strong set of links with Lions Club, the Canal and Rivers Trust who look after the Grand Union Canal, our local wards and Ealing Council. This bodes well for bringing neglected green spaces back into use, possibly as community gardens using permaculture principles to grow food in a sustainable manner. It is through these types of partnerships that we can attract more volunteers since more help is always welcome. The need for more locally grown produce was made even clearer during the pandemic when many people had to resort to food banks and charities to feed themselves and Incredible Edible Southall is providing one demonstrable way to contribute to that community need.

Through working together across many organisations to establish beds, and then through agreements to care for them, we have strong educational links with local schools and nurseries (for children, not plants!), are all permanently engaged with Incredible Edible Southall since we have raised beds in common. These interlinked activities can only provide bedrock upon which to build educational channels that go both ways.

Our gardens and orchards show how our landscape could be used to supply fresh organic produce to local businesses and charities. As we grow our volunteer force, dig more deeply into the growing culture of many of our residents, continue to foster good relationships across the community, and as our orchards and beds mature, we are confident in our capacity to tap more and more into mutually beneficial community and commercial relationships.

50% COMMUNITY

40% LEARNING

10% BUSINESS

SOUTHALL

ULVERSTON
ENGLAND

WHERE

Ulverston market town received its charter in 1280 and was first recorded as Ulurestun in the Domesday Book of 1086. Just outside the Lake District National Park in Cumbria, it is only a mile from the sea. The combination of cobbled streets, independent shops, and many annual festivals, attracts visitors year round. It has over three hundred allotments and several parks, including Ford Park, the only community-owned park in the UK.

WHO

Incredible Edible Ulverston, under the guidance of Kim Farr, works in a loose network with Ulverston Town Council, Ulverston in Bloom, Ulverston Food Waste Project, Garden Organic's Master Composters, Ford Park, Gill Banks Action Group (woodland conservation) and many others to grow and share food.

WHAT

Incredible Edible Ulverston and Ulverston in Bloom organise, plant and maintain over one hundred and twenty tubs, troughs, boats, gardens and flower beds around the town as well as giving some support to other groups. We plant herbs, edible flowers, strawberries, fruit bushes, crab apple trees, trees and shrubs with berries, amongst the general planting, as well as having some dedicated edible planting spots. We have reduced the planting of annuals, and have moved to perennials only in all permanent planting areas. We recycle the plants and compost from the seasonal tubs.

RECIPE FOR COMPOST

From our Master Composter Steve Povey comes this guide for a three bay open system made with 10 wooden pallets.

· Choose a shady corner and build straight onto the ground.
· Fix the pallets together upright in three open topped continuous squares, using nails, strong wire or strong string.
· In front of each square make a pallet door, hinged on one side with strong wire.
· Stuff cardboard into each pallet side as insulation.
· Paint bay numbers on them – Bay 1, Bay 2, Bay 3.

Fill Bay 1 using any organic material (grass, veg peelings, fruit scraps, tea bags, coffee grounds, old plants, etc). Bulk out these green fillings with brown stuff (paper, card, leaves, wood ash, straw, etc). Use a 50/50 mix of greens and browns. Avoid non-organic materials (stone, metal, plastic, etc) also perennial weeds and coal ash. Also crumple any paper or card to leave air for the worms to breathe. When Bay 1 is full, start filling Bay 3. When Bay 3 is half full, mix Bay 1 and Bay 3 together into Bay 2. Begin the process again by filling Bay 1. Use a garden fork to stir the contents of Bay 2 weekly. After 3-6 months you will have wonderful peat free, smell free and cost free compost for your plants in Bay 2 for use as soil improver, growing medium and as a mulch.

Mix for hanging baskets, tubs and large plant pots:
· A bucket of home-made peat free compost
· A handful of fish, blood and bone (as long term food)
· A handful of grit/sand (to improve drainage - Adjust amount accordingly)
· A teaspoon of water retaining crystals
· Mix thoroughly and remove lumps.
· Put into container and plant up.

> "PERHAPS OUR GREATEST ACHIEVEMENT IS HOW WE HAVE CREATED A CULTURE OF WORKING TOGETHER, LARGELY AS A DIRECT RESULT OF GOOD COMMUNICATION.

TIPS

· Be organised. We have a bank account, chair, secretary, treasurer and constitution, all of which helps with applying for grants. A weekly email goes out with what we are doing and where and any news updates.

· Be assertive. There was a small patch of grass with a seat next to a pub. We couldn't find out who owned it so we planted fruit trees there. There was a large area of ground alongside some steps from a big car park down to the shops which was scruffy and full of litter and needles. We asked who owned it and even went to the council planning consultants to check ownership. Apparently, no-one owns it, so with initial help from the Scouts we have turned it into a mixture of flower gardens, soft fruit production and a mini-nature reserve and it looks beautiful!

· Ask for help and work with others.
  · We got 60 Brownies through their Gardening Badge as a way to involve them.
  · The local hospice asked for a kick start for their kitchen garden.
  · We helped the Food Technology teacher at the High School by part funding and setting up tubs for herbs for cooking for his students.
  · A local school asked for help with a Butterfly Garden.

· Support the local council to meet their climate change/biodiversity targets.

· Raise your profile by getting in the local press, having an interesting facebook page that gets shared, and getting on local radio – people then know who you are and can ask for help or for a flower display or volunteer.

· Communicate with other projects that are involved in similar activities and make them part of your entries to the regional (Cumbria in Bloom) or national Britain In Bloom competitions in the UK.

· Organise Open Garden weekends or gardening competitions and reward food growing and nature friendly gardening with prizes.

STORIES

We've been successful at tying ourselves into local events. We filled the town with the suffragette colours at the centenary of women getting the vote. We had red, white and blue displays for the Royal Airforce and Royal British Legion centenaries. When the Tour of Britain Cycle Race came we put bikes around the town with baskets on them full of flowers. The key to all of this is planning in advance. Each summer we choose a colour scheme for the next year, research the flowering plants suitable for planters and which will welcome pollinators. That information is shared with the local nursery to ensure that their tendency to produce plants that are easy to grow is balanced by our needs to have plants where insects can access the flowers. We have more tiered planters and troughs full of colour over the summer and autumn months, but make a big effort to look good all year for our festival, theatre, and cinema visitors. Recently we have been developing five mini-nature reserves across the town with quality composting bays, bug hotels, beetle buckets, dead hedges, a pond, bird boxes, hedgehog houses, wildflowers and bird feeders.

Organisations within the networked group also do excellent work such as The Friends of Lightburn Park. They work with a local school for children with special needs, and plant up raised beds with Incredible Edible in the park. The town council support us with grants and arrange eco-fairs, World Environment Day events, and allotment prizes. They organised a sell out talk (600+ people) by Professor Mike Berners-Lee, the author of "There is no Planet B". Ford Park grow flowers, fruit and vegetables in their walled garden and greenhouse, train volunteers and run a small nursery selling everything from tomato and kale plants to interesting perennials. Volunteers feel themselves to be valued members of the team and the community. We don't waste their time and they know what we are doing.

Our commitment to communications and PR runs deep:

· We run a joint facebook page for Incredible Edible Ulverston, Ulverston in Bloom and the Gill Banks Action Group which has over 800 followers and a reach of 3K+. A post about negotiating a break in mowing a lawn by a community centre, which allowed two species of orchid to flourish, created lots of comment and a reached 3+K. As a great biodiversity story it was picked up by the South Lakeland News. As a result the local press and radio journalists keep an eye on the facebook page.

· We reciprocate news support from others by including a few educational posts on our facebook page from Cumbria Wildlife Trust or the Royal Horticultural Society about making compost or wildlife friendly gardening.

· Ulverston has its own digital station CANDO FM. We are always ready with details and photos if asked.

· We ourselves write articles that are not time critical, and the papers are grateful for copy for a slow news day!

· We make sure to attend all relevant events with a stall or a presentation to raise our profile, and talk to the public when we are gardening around the town every Wednesday morning.

· Every interaction provides an opportunity to promote Incredible Edible.

55%

COMMUNITY

We work with schools, the local Hospice, a residential home for people with dementia, the parish church, allotment holders, social housing, youth groups and others. "It is all about connection," says Kim. "Many volunteers work in more than one group so we think 2+2=5!". Working together and making friends means everyone's skills, and every hour given, is valuable. All the different projects that work across the town are doing something slightly different – the allotments with wildflower areas; a pond; organic gardening at The Plot; the council with their tree and hedge planting targets; groups of families in social housing called Sophie's Garden. People want to feel that they belong to something, so it's great that the Gill Banks Action Group meet on a Sunday morning, Incredible Edible Ulverston & Ulverston in Bloom on Wednesday mornings, while Ford Park's volunteering days are Tuesday and Thursday. Working together keeps our many disparate volunteers interconnected, from people who are retired or work part-time to those with learning difficulties. Working together means communities can grow. There is more help, people bring in others, established groups can back up new groups in their bids for support, competitions can be entered jointly, be won, and the winnings shared, as happened when the Lord Cavendish Cup for "Greening the Grey" was won by Sophie's Garden. A local business gave a greenhouse and the Mayor gave a grant.

25%

LEARNING

We all learn from each other in terms of plant identification, how to make a good compost, how to grow and what other volunteering opportunities are around. Some formal courses are run in horticulture and we advertise both face to face courses in things such as permaculture, mushroom growing, and composting, as well as webinars on topics like nature recovery and creating a wildflower meadow. We also encourage citizen science through events like the Royal Society for the Protection of Birds, Big Garden Birdwatch, and the Butterfly Conservation's Big Butterfly Count. The main thrust of much of what we do is to educate the local community about gardening, food waste and composting, to conserve and develop local woodland with more native species, to reduce the use of chemicals, and to promote biodiversity.

We get considerable financial support from local businesses including fees for putting a sign on a roundabout, an annual grant from the Ulverston Business Improvement District Group, one-off grant support from a local publishing group for planting up a new car park, and being a cause for a year with The Co-operative group retail arm. We feel we have a rôle to make the town look beautiful and to support local businesses. We focus on the town centre, the bus stops, the station, and car parks, as this is where visitors arrive. We are very keen to make our local environment beautiful, and to enhance shopping, dining, and staying locally, which is good for the local economy and for the environment.

We are appreciated. For one example, in return for our efforts a local pub owner and property developer uses his car and a bowser to water all our planters once a week throughout the summer. For another, many people come to pick the fruit and herbs in town and one greengrocer has asked us to plant more rosemary to go with Sunday roasts as she is sending all her customers to the herb bed opposite. The possibilities of more symbiotic relationships between us and the business community are exciting.

20%

BUSINESS

ULVERSTON

PART THREE

POINTING A WAY

MARK WEBSTER
MANAGING DIRECTOR, ESS

ESS is the Defence, Energy and Government Services sector of Compass Group UK & Ireland. Compass is the largest food and support services company in the UK and we employ tens of thousands of people, operating in over 6,000 locations across a variety of sectors.

As part of a multinational corporation, we're people powered and are made up of individuals who are concerned about the future of our planet.

We know that if you add all food-related emissions together, including livestock, farming, deforestation and food waste, then what we eat and drink ranks number one in the greatest causes of global warming, along with the energy supply sector[1].

Our food system is contributing to a climate crisis as well as a crisis of nature. In Incredible Edible we have found visionary, generous people looking to address both.

The Incredible Edible groups have created sustainable community food systems across the globe for more than a decade. They have demonstrated how to have an impact at a hyper-localised level, recognising the importance of working together, learning and enterprise.

I was lucky enough to visit the Conwy Incredible Edible team and meet with volunteers from several other sites. The passion for initiating change was clear to see, as was the importance of the work for the local community with beautiful, thoughtfully laid out and informative planted areas spread across the town. Particularly impressive was the approach to engagement and education. I loved the signage explaining how to use the ingredients and the simple descriptions about the benefits of each.

What a joy for the Incredible Edible members to grow amazing food and share their knowledge

> **I'M EXCITED ABOUT HOW WE CAN WORK WITH INCREDIBLE EDIBLE TO PROMOTE THE USE OF THE PRODUCTS WE ARE GROWING AND ENCOURAGE MORE PEOPLE TO GET INVOLVED IN TRANSFORMING AND EATING THEIR LANDSCAPES!**

[1]*Drawdown. The Most Comprehensive Plan Ever Proposed to Reverse Global Warming. Paul Hawken.*

on the best ways to cook and eat it – my team and I found it truly inspiring! Anything we can do to offer meaningful support is a privilege in its truest sense.

Within ESS we are building a series of community gardens across our estate. We are fortunate that our defence and government clients are located on large sites that often have land to spare. Many customers live and work on base and there is a strong sense of community between military personnel, civil servants and our colleagues. These factors combine to give us the potential to do something special for the benefit of all which is where the idea for growing and using our own ingredients was born.

We have a lot to learn from Incredible Edible as we look to extend the model across our business!

Our first project is at Brompton Barracks in Chatham, home to the Royal School of Military Engineering, where we provide catering and a range of other facilities services. We've built an allotment on site where we grow a variety of fruit, vegetables and herbs. Our chefs use the products in their day-to-day menus, as well as during fine dining functions. This really shines a light on the ingredients, sparking a keen interest from our customers. We've also installed planters alongside outdoor seating which improves the appeal of the areas, encouraging people to relax and socialise around the food we are growing.

Royal Engineers Association veterans look after the allotments and have provided great feedback on the mental health benefits associated with being part of the project. We maintain a wormery on site that processes food waste into nutrient dense compost and three beehives that produced 40kg of honey this year!

We are an organisation full of people who are passionate about great food. Our culinary teams pride themselves on showcasing great, locally sourced ingredients and teaching others how to use them. I'm excited about how we can work with Incredible Edible to promote the use of the products we are growing and encourage more people to get involved in transforming and eating their landscapes!

"AS PART OF A MULTINATIONAL CORPORATION, WE'RE PEOPLE POWERED AND ARE MADE UP OF INDIVIDUALS WHO ARE CONCERNED ABOUT THE FUTURE OF OUR PLANET.

CAROLYN BALL

DIRECTOR FOR DELIVERY OF NET ZERO, COMPASS GROUP UK & IRELAND

I love Incredible Edible.

The groups celebrated through these pages are not just growing food. Their existence recognises that climate change has a human face and together they inspire everyday actions we can all support.

In many ways it is a masterclass in how food can unite communities through small changes that can be scaled.

In being so, it is also a movement about economics; calling for a transformation in the value of food so we have a system fit to serve the future - and all those who will inherit it.

Anything we can do to support the groups is a privilege and we look forward to sharing learnings, joy and radical generosity at such a critical time.

May this focus continue to be a tonic for the soul and a bright light for society.

With sleeves firmly rolled-up and in solidarity always,

Carolyn.

"INCREDIBLE EDIBLE IS A MASTERCLASS IN HOW FOOD CAN UNITE COMMUNITIES THROUGH SMALL CHANGES THAT CAN BE SCALED.

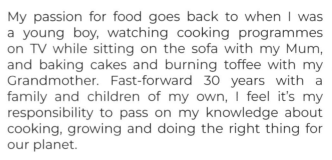

SCOTT FREEMAN
CULINARY DIRECTOR, ESS

"**I KNOW I CAN'T FIX THE CLIMATE CHALLENGES AS A SINGLE PERSON BUT I CAN HELP IN MY OWN WAY.**

My passion for food goes back to when I was a young boy, watching cooking programmes on TV while sitting on the sofa with my Mum, and baking cakes and burning toffee with my Grandmother. Fast-forward 30 years with a family and children of my own, I feel it's my responsibility to pass on my knowledge about cooking, growing and doing the right thing for our planet.

I am an avid amateur gardener and grower, but my success can be very hit or miss at times! I try to produce some of my own fruit, vegetables and herbs and get my children involved so they understand more about our food chain and the enjoyment that can come from growing a tiny seed into something you eventually get to eat a few months down the line. I love foraging in the surrounding countryside where I live and have a few secret spots of my own that I revisit throughout the year to enjoy some free wild food. I have a walnut tree in my back garden that I share with the local squirrel population – there is always enough to share between us!

We eat with the seasons and one of my favourite things is visiting my local Pick Your Own in the spring to pick the first of the asparagus, and in the summer our glorious strawberry and raspberry harvests and the big red smiles on my girls' faces as we walk through the fruit fields. As a chef, I have a great respect for all ingredients and still enjoy meat, game and poultry, but source this locally and steer clear of mass-produced options. I like keeping my local economy thriving as well as the interaction between the butcher, farmers and myself.

In recent years, with our awareness of our impact on the climate through our eating preferences, I would now say that at least half of my meals are plant-based or vegetarian, sometimes more. This isn't a conscious effort either – with rising food costs it's cheaper, quicker and often my children prefer these meals anyway. I know I can't fix the climate challenges as a single person but I can help in my own way.

I met Pam in Conwy in 2021 after watching her TED talk on YouTube. She is an honest talking, no-nonsense person who has inspired many with an amazing movement that is achievable throughout every city, town and village with a little can-do. Walking through the beautiful town and seeing fresh herbs and vegetables growing outside the police station, by traffic lights and either side of the church doors was fantastic, and I cannot wait to re-visit. The influence and dedication of just a few people in this community has literally transformed dull areas of a beautiful town into something truly incredible.

Within ESS, we are fortunate that several of our clients are freeing up spaces for us to grow a range of produce on site. I've used some of the ingredients being grown at RSME Brompton Barracks to create the following recipes. Give them a try – I hope you enjoy them!

SHAKSHOUKA WITH CHARRED CABBAGE, TOASTED WILD GARLIC BREAD AND ROASTED NEW POTATOES

For the shakshouka

This baked egg dish is a family favourite in my house and is so easy to make. We eat it at breakfast, lunch or dinner and it's quick to prepare, nutritious and cheap to make. This recipe pairs up really well with some homemade bread, toasted and slathered with the wild garlic butter and dunked into the sauce.

Serves 4

Ingredients:
- 1 small onion
- 2 cloves garlic
- 1 pepper
- 1 tbsp olive oil
- 1 tsp cumin seeds
- 1 tsp fennel seeds
- 2 tsp smoked paprika
- 2 tbsp tomato puree
- 500g freshly grown tomatoes (including green ones if you have a glut)
- 2 tbsp chopped coriander
- 4 eggs (8 if you are really hungry!)
- Sea salt flakes and freshly ground pepper to taste

Method:
1. Finely dice the onion, pepper and garlic and cook slowly in a pan with the olive oil until they are transparent.
2. Lightly toast the cumin and fennel seeds and grind to a fine powder – then add this to the onion and pepper mixture along with the smoked paprika and the tomato puree. Continue to cook on a low heat for a few more minutes, being careful to not burn the puree.
3. Finely chop your fresh tomatoes and then add them to the pan making sure all of the juice goes in too. Allow the tomatoes to cook down into the sauce slowly – this will take another few minutes. You may need to add a drop of water if the sauce gets too thick at this stage.
4. Spread the sauce around your pan and make some indentations which you will then crack your eggs into. Cover the pan with a lid and cook for a further 3 minutes on a low heat.
5. Chop your coriander and sprinkle on top just before serving with your charred cabbage, wild garlic toast and new potatoes.

For the charred cabbage:

Growing up, I used to hate cabbage – it was often boiled and was always the last vegetable to be eaten on my plate. By charring, the cabbage takes on a different flavour and retains some of the crunch, which makes it much more appealing. I haven't had much success with growing my own cabbages – the caterpillars and butterflies seem to love them – but I try every year all the same.

Ingredients:
- 1 hispi cabbage (preferably home-grown)
- 1 tbsp olive oil
- Salt and freshly ground pepper to taste

Method:
1. Heat a griddle or heavy based pan until it is very hot.
2. Wash and thoroughly dry your cabbage and then cut it into wedges, dependant on how big your cabbage is.
3. Rub the olive oil all over the cabbage and then season liberally with the sea-salt flakes and freshly ground pepper.
4. Grill the cabbage on all sides until well-charred, then place into a bowl and cover with a cloth until you are ready to eat. The steam from the charring will continue to help cook the cabbage perfectly.

For the wild garlic butter:
I'm lucky enough to have my own supply of free wild garlic growing in my garden that makes a welcome appearance every spring. My family love the taste and we use it nearly every day in our meals for a few months until the flowers turn to seed, at which point I steep these in extra virgin olive oil and use later in the year when my supply of wild garlic butter runs out. This recipe for wild garlic butter goes well with toast, bruschetta and for glazing your Sunday roast vegetables.

Makes about 300 grams or two well rolled cylinders

Ingredients:
- 250g salted butter
- 50g wild garlic leaves (a few very big handfuls)
- 1 teaspoon freshly cracked black pepper

Method:
1. Remove the butter from the fridge and allow it to soften naturally – resist the urge to microwave or melt the butter as this will be very messy later on!
2. Wash and pat dry the wild garlic leaves. Place them into a liquidiser with about 50g of the butter and puree on high speed until the leaves are pureed and turn a vivid bright green.
3. Add the remaining softened butter and the black pepper and continue to puree until really smooth and bright green.
4. Take a sheet of greaseproof paper and place half of the garlic butter into the middle of the sheet. Roll the butter into a level cylinder and repeat with the other half.
5. You can now freeze the butter for when you need it or keep it in the fridge and use it within a few days.

For the roasted new potatoes with wild garlic butter:
One of my favourite memories as a child was when my Grandad would come to my house with bags of potatoes that he had grown in his allotment. We boiled them with huge bunches of mint and ate them with butter. This recipe uses the wild garlic butter from my previous recipe.

Ingredients:
- 250g new potatoes – preferably freshly dug from the garden
- 2 tbsp sunflower oil
- Sea salt flakes and freshly ground black pepper
- 2 tbsp wild garlic butter

Method:
1. If the potatoes are quite big, cut them in half otherwise keep them whole.
2. Rub them all over with the salt, pepper and oil.
3. Bake in an oven at 200 degrees C for about 30 mins, turning occasionally.
4. Once cooked, add the wild garlic butter and coat the potatoes before serving.

"AT RMSE BROMPTON, WE HAVE THREE COLONIES OF BEES WHICH PRODUCE THE MOST INCREDIBLE HONEY.

HEDGEROW SUMMER PUDDING WITH HONEY ICE CREAM

I love foraging in the summer and autumn – garden-grown and wild berries, plums, elderberries, and apples all make this pudding naturally sweet and a simple yet impressive dessert. I have a 'secret' foraging spot that every year produces the most amazing tiny wild raspberries that always go into this recipe. At RMSE Brompton, we have three colonies of bees which produce the most incredible honey. This sweetens the pudding and also makes for a nice drizzle over the ice cream just before serving.

Serves 4

Ingredients:
500g mixed berries – Raspberries, blackcurrants, blueberries, redcurrants – whatever you have grown and have a glut of
1 big Bramley apple
100g sugar
50g honey
Several slices of white bread – either homemade or sliced

Method:
1. Prepare a bowl (I use my Christmas pudding bowl) by lining it with clingfilm.
2. Place the berries and half of the sugar into a small saucepan and simmer very gently until the berries soften and become liquidy. Set this to one side to cool.
3. Peel and core the apple and place in a saucepan with the remaining sugar and a drop of water and cook slowly until the apple has softened and can be mashed easily. Set aside to cool.
4. Remove the crusts from your bread and set to one side. Cut one disk for the base of the bowl and a bigger one for the top.
5. Puree half of the berry mixture and pour into a deep sided dish and submerge your bread slices into the liquid thoroughly.
6. Place the smaller disc into the base of the bowl and then the slices around the outside, patching any broken pieces as you go.
7. Mix the remaining berries with the apples and half of the honey and place this into the bowl.
8. Put the larger disk on the top of the bowl and cover with the clingfilm.
9. Place this into the fridge and put something heavy on top for 24 hours to allow the bread to totally soak up all the fruit juices.
10. To serve, use the very best ice-cream you can find (I use a local diary that makes amazing milk ice cream) and leave out at room temperature for an hour. Beat in the remaining half of the honey and put back into the freezer until you are ready to serve.
11. Remove the summer pudding from the bowl, discard the clingfilm, add a big scoop of the honey ice cream on top and enjoy!

PART FOUR

NEXT STEPS

HUGH ELLIS

CHANGING THE LAW

We know that local food can transform people's lives for the better. The Incredible Edible model has shown how local food growing can bring people together to reduce loneliness, connect with nature, combat climate change, and provide healthy diets.

But there's a simple problem. Communities are being held back by a lack of land for local food. The desire and ambition is there, but without land communities simply can't crack on with the positive change that we all need after the pandemic. This land problem reveals a wider issue for communities about how much power they actually have to make change happen in their neighbourhoods. Incredible Edible wants to solve the problem by promoting a new Act of Parliament that would give communities a right to grow on public sector owned land.

I started my life as a community campaigner, trained as a town planner, ended up working in the sterile world of Westminster policy. Then I finally found my way back to the inspirational ideas of self-help and Community Action which founded the planning movement. Along the way it became clear that land and the wealth it generates sits at the heart of our economy and of our politics. The question is whether land should solely benefit its owners or be put to work for the wider benefit of communities?

There's nothing new in this question. From the English Civil War, to the theft of land through the enclosure movement, and on to Highland clearances, arguments have raged about why ordinary people are denied the most basic land rights. The debate changed after 1947 when the Labour government introduced comprehensive planning based on local councils. They nationalised the right to develop land and gave most decisions to elected representatives. The system produced some triumphs and it also made mistakes. Over time the system became more and more captured by private sector

Board member and director of Incredible Edible CIC.

Hugh is Policy Director of the Town and Country Planning Association, and heads policy development, briefings and engagement with central government and politicians. He led the secretariat for the Raynsford Review in 2018 and campaigns on land reform, the climate crisis and health. Since 2015, Hugh has co-authored four books – 'Rebuilding Britain', 'Town Planning in Crisis', 'The Art of Building a Garden City' and New Towns: the rise, fall and rebirth.

"INCREDIBLE EDIBLE WANTS TO SOLVE THE PROBLEM BY PROMOTING A NEW ACT OF PARLIAMENT THAT WOULD GIVE COMMUNITIES A RIGHT TO GROW ON PUBLIC SECTOR OWNED LAND.

development interests and there's been growing anger that there is a lack of real community participation in decisions. Even so, the system muddled through until, in the last decade, rounds of deregulation broke the legitimacy of the English planning system.

What happens to land is now decisively in the hands of landowners. This is a problem because their motivations rarely align with the kinds of post pandemic actions we need to achieve on health and climate change. In some cases, it's a simple problem of landowners extracting value that should be recycled in the local community. In other cases, it's about landowners doing nothing with their land but resting on its increasing speculative value. For the public sector it is often about having no money to invest positively in the land it does own. In some towns I visit no one seems to know who owns chunks of neglected green space. Urgent action is needed on climate and health inequalities, people are demanding more say over the decision that affect them. Taken together the pressure is growing for a new approach.

The frustrating thing is that the land is there – underused verges, land waiting for development, land which is simply derelict. A lot of this land is in public sector ownership and is either costly to manage or not managed at all. Where communities have the resources and the opportunity they can enter into leases or even buy small pieces of land. But for most community food growers that aspiration is out of reach. What we need is a simple way for communities to access land which is cheap and doesn't involve lengthy and complicated legal agreements or expensive obligation to fence and gate land before growing can begin.

We know there is plenty of land that could be used for local growing. So our objective is simple – how can we make a new law to speed up and simplify access to land for community growing?

The answer is to give people a right to grow on 'suitable' public sector land. Why just public sector? Because this is best place to start because public sector bodies have some level of accountability and, you would hope, some sense of corporate social responsibility. And why a new law? Simply because that most powerful way of getting the big enabling change we need. Our proposed new law would do just that and create a sensible and balanced system which can transform the look and feel of our communities. We all know the plots of land in our community which could be permanently, or just for a few years, made available for growing. This new law would create opportunities for communities to come together to make the very best use of public sector land. With the drive to build back better, this is an idea whose time has come.

It's important to say up front that we understand that communities need much more than new laws if they're going to thrive. The morale of the local community and some cash to get started are probably the most important ingredients of success, but this new law would deal with one of the major blockages to progress and enable much greater levels of local action. The legislation is based around two simple principles.

Asking local authorities to identify on a map all public sector land which is suitable for growing or environmental enhancement.

Creating a simple process whereby communities can apply to cultivate this land for a defined period without the need for a formal lease or complex license.

The provisions of our proposed new law would:

Create a legal duty on local authorities, District and Unitary councils and London Boroughs, to publish a list of land held by all public authorities which is suitable for community cultivation or environmental enhancement. We are still working through how wide this list would be, but it would include local authorities and all Government departments and agencies including the NHS. It might also include water utilities. The presumption would be that all this land is suitable for cultivation or environmental enhancement unless there is a clear and demonstrable reason why not.

Create a right to cultivate land on the list through a certificate of lawful use. The community can

> **COMMUNITIES ARE BEING HELD BACK BY A LACK OF LAND FOR LOCAL FOOD. THE DESIRE AND AMBITION IS THERE, BUT WITHOUT LAND COMMUNITIES SIMPLY CAN'T CRACK ON WITH THE POSITIVE CHANGE THAT WE ALL NEED AFTER THE PANDEMIC.**

"FROM THE ENGLISH CIVIL WAR, TO THE THEFT OF LAND THROUGH THE ENCLOSURE MOVEMENT, AND ON TO HIGHLAND CLEARANCES, ARGUMENTS HAVE RAGED ABOUT WHY ORDINARY PEOPLE ARE DENIED THE MOST BASIC LAND RIGHTS.

apply for this certificate at any time and, once issued by the local authority, they can cultivate the land for the agreed period. There would be no change in the ownership of the land and no rental charge would be applied.

Communities would be able nominate land for the list if they felt the council had missed an important asset.

Once on the list the land can't be disposed of for a defined period and the community has the right to bid for the land if it's being sold.

Communities could use the land for food growing or environmental enhancement. This ensures that land which may be unsuitable for cultivation because of contamination could be used for non-food gardening or bee keeping.

Public authorities would be able to refuse to include public sector land if they can show it is going to be used to for other public interest objectives, like social housing, within a period of 24 months.

This new law would not be a perfect solution because there will be arguments about what 'suitable for cultivation' means. However, by creating a duty to map land suitable for growing AND environmental enhancement, it reduces the scope to say 'no' and reveals the scale of local possibilities. This will happen by us doing our best to persuade parliamentarians to support this measure and by building a coalition of partners who will help bring pressure to bear on the Government to support this legislation. Government has to enable the change to make local food growing blossom. Let's reconnect people with the land and make our communities healthy and green.

JANIE BICKERSTETH

HUNGRY FOR CHANGE

My earliest veg patch memory was when I was nine, helping my dad meticulously thin out some seedling carrots. When the plants matured, we discovered they were not carrots at all but the beautiful flower 'Love in a Mist'! It was one of those treasured moments I had with my dad - that we had spent so long working to improve our chances of a bumper carrot crop but instead, we had a veg patch filled with flowers... Yet, how lucky I was to grow up with a dad who taught me how to grow veg, working by his side; experiential learning has always been the best way for me. Growing food truly was, and continues to be, an 'incredible' experience; to plant a tiny seed and watch it grow - or watch it get munched by snails, slugs, pigeons or sat on by my dog. So many elements can go wrong, but, in a way, that's the constant challenge and thrill of the annual process - there's always next year to get it right.

Incredible Edible was first on my radar around 2012, after Pam hit the headlines with that TED Talk. I loved the name - it made me smile. I also loved the simplicity of the message, and I loved the energy of Pam - her 'can do' approach. For several years, I had been trying to grow veg with children at my kids' primary school in Durham. If only I had had the Incredible Edible concept to refer to, I think the veg growing would have taken off ten times faster. In 2013 our family moved to Singapore, where I established an Incredible Edible in a school with over 3,000 students, and that is when I really embraced the idea of the three plates. It wasn't enough simply to grow the food, what we needed to do was change hearts and minds, we needed to get people thinking about how they could get food to market, to close the loop. The children made pesto from the huge basil crop, we dried moringa and sold it as a superfood to all the yoga mums. Today, the veg patch is thriving and the gardening group makes dill oil to sell. It was great for the children to hold money in their hands, to see that all that hard slog of growing veg could generate some income. For me, there was nothing more

Board member and director of Incredible Edible CIC.

Janie is an artist, potter, writer, and mother. She co-founded an Incredible Edible in Singapore and, until July 2021, was chair of Incredible Edible Lambeth. She has spent a career bringing artistry to issues around food, education and sustainability.

> **"THIS IS THE ESSENCE OF INCREDIBLE EDIBLE – A MODEL OF THE THREE SPINNING PLATES – STRONG, RESILIENT COMMUNITIES HELPING EACH OTHER TO PROVIDE HEALTHY, NUTRITIOUS, AFFORDABLE LOCAL FOOD, TO GENERATE ENOUGH FOOD FOR BUSINESSES TO FLOW FROM THIS, AND TO SUPPORT LEARNING SO THAT EVERYONE REALISES HOW LIFE-ENHANCING IT CAN BE TO GROW YOUR OWN FOOD.**

important than transferring my accumulated veg growing knowledge to those children.

Fast forward to 2021 and I found myself running Incredible Edible Lambeth - an early adopter of Incredible Edible, notwithstanding it's in inner city London, where green space around housing estates has been largely managed for minimum effort through harsh mowing and pruning regimes. Even so, there are hundreds of people growing food in backyards, on balconies, and in community gardens and allotments. The original Incredible Edible 'can do' concept continues to inspire, to support, and enable more people to grow food. In Lambeth our efforts are being noticed; food growing improves participants' mental and physical health, and regenerates degraded spaces. Our local authority is beginning to recognise how significant the changes could be if they allowed more community growing throughout the borough. They know that Incredible Edible can be a gateway for them, but they are a little nervous of letting people have agency over the land on their estates. It's uncertain territory, it's messy, it's disorganised, but it means that people come together outdoors to grow food and that simple act can be truly transformational; this is happening in hundreds of thousands of places all over the world, where people come together to grow, to cook, to share.

So, what's next? Change is afoot – fast and drastic change is needed and, post-pandemic, perhaps there is finally momentum for that change. Across London and other metropolitan centres, people are disconnected from farming and nature; in a small but significant way, the Incredible Edible movement is making those connections between food, farming and nature meaningful, particularly for low income households living on estates, with limited access to land. I'd like to see community gardens on every housing estate, providing residents with an opportunity to grow food, often for the first time, with community composting of kitchen waste enriching soils and raising awareness of the wastefulness of contemporary life. I have seen first hand how these gardens can heal disconnected communities, bringing people together to share a previously neglected green space right on their doorstep.

This experience in Lambeth has led me to think more broadly about ownership and access to land. At a national level, institutions as varied as the NHS, the Church of England, and many of the utility companies steward large tracts of land. What if these institutions loaned a percentage of their land to people who want to grow food? What if the Church of England were to get behind Incredible Edible's proposed Rights to Grow bill, where land is offered to local communities to manage for increased food growing and biodiversity? Could we start to reverse the catastrophic decline in our insect population? Could we begin to grow even a small percentage of our food needs, reducing our dependence on a wasteful, carbon-heavy international food system.

Many of us changed our shopping habits in 2020/2021, as our horizons narrowed during lockdown and we looked to support local enterprises. Young people are re-assessing - they seem hungry for change, disillusioned with the daily commute, many are looking for peri-urban land to grow food, but this remains very hard to come by. We need our government to get behind this groundswell who are eager for new ways of working; providing financial incentives for landowners to release land for farm starts. We need policies and financial incentives that support small farmers to grow food where it is most needed, food that is close to or within cities. We need more food growing in secondary schools, more horticultural training, a job creation programme for young people to grow food, and from there, small food and drinks businesses will begin to emerge. This is the essence of Incredible Edible - a model of the three spinning plates - strong, resilient communities helping each other to provide nutritious, affordable local food, to generate enough food for businesses to flow from this, and to support learning so that everyone realises how life-enhancing it can be to grow your own food.

The Incredible Edible slogan "If you eat, you're in" says it all. Everyone is welcome to join this much needed, long overdue transformation of our food system. I'm thrilled to be taking part in this food revolution.

THE INCREDIBLE EDIBLE SLOGAN "IF YOU EAT, YOU'RE IN" SAYS IT ALL.

GARY STOTT

INTO THE FUTURE

Every time I think about Incredible Edible – the people I have met, the groups I have visited and the places that I've been – it is almost impossible not to be reminded of the words of Margaret Mead, "Never doubt that a small group of thoughtful, committed citizens can change the world; indeed, it's the only thing that ever has." In the same thought I am provoked to ask the question, what does it mean to 'change the world'?

It is true that Incredible Edible has had a profound effect on thousands of lives since the first group of pioneers dreamed of a different world thirteen years ago. For each person who has seen an example or heard a story of people making change, that impact has been profoundly personal and local.

Part of the power of Incredible Edible is that it was not based upon a manifesto, upon a vision statement, or upon mission principles, but upon a story. A story which has been told, and a story which has been acted out. People saw others in villages, towns and cities doing things which inspired them towards a shared future that they also hoped for, and they saw in those small actions something that they felt would be achievable. The story was told, one to another, and people copied and improvised and made the story their own.

There can be challenges with this type of growth for a movement. Stories have a tremendous power in human history and they have that power precisely because stories resonate with something that is already within us, with a truth buried, just waiting for a spark to bring it into flame. Everyone who hears the story of Incredible Edible focuses on the thing that matters the most to them and this means that sometimes Incredible Edible groups across the UK look very different to each other. This is not just okay, this is to be celebrated and amplified. Each citizen activist, in their own way, believes that through

Board member and former Executive Director of Incredible Edible CIC.

Gary is a social entrepreneur, co-founder and Chair of Community Shop CIC and Executive Director of Arena Partners. He is a former homelessness CEO, regional advisor on homelessness and a recipient of the Prime Minister's Big Society Award.

> **"PART OF THE POWER OF INCREDIBLE EDIBLE IS THAT IT WAS NOT BASED UPON A MANIFESTO, UPON A VISION STATEMENT, OR UPON MISSION PRINCIPLES, BUT UPON A STORY. A STORY WHICH HAS BEEN TOLD, AND A STORY WHICH HAS BEEN ACTED OUT.**

their small actions they can build kind, confident and connected communities through the power of food, and that it comes through passionately engaging in community and learning and business.

And so each of us, in our own way, and in every community, magnifies the Incredible Edible story in order to make change visible. And again, that inspires in me the question what does it mean to change the world? For some of us the horizons of our world are the four or five people who live in our street with whom we share the day-to-day joys and troubles of life. For some of us it is the communal use of our town and it's public spaces. For some of us it is the local food economy and local businesses. For some it is issues of justice and sovereignty around food. Each in our own way scans the horizon that means most to us and longs for change now, and for a better future.

Over the years since Incredible Edible was born there has been an increasing focus on 'systems change', indeed it has become popular and fashionable. It has become part of the curriculum in some academic departments and, in anchor institutions, like Local Authorities, there is often a systems change specialist or even a whole team. For me that focus on systems change is valuable and important. Incredible Edible, at our best, is not about a group of like-minded people forming an exclusive club to affirm our views of the world and of each other. It is about a movement for change so that all people in all communities will be able to live thriving and prosperous lives – lives with good, healthy, local food, lives with good quality housing, education, and jobs. Incredible Edible is about growing but it is always about growing the circumstances where a human being can fulfil their potential within the place that they called home. This living of a prosperous life is not defined by economic metrics but by the whole range of social, environmental and human capital.

The need for us to change our direction and to live within planetary boundaries has become even more amplified in the last few years. I think that the Incredible Edible model of systems change will always, inevitably, be a unique expression of people powered change. Now with one hundred and fifty groups across the UK and thousands around the world we learn more and more each day from listening to each other and seeing what makes change possible, attractive and beneficial in our local communities. Incredible Edible's model of systems change will always be about harnessing the shared wisdom of grassroots change-makers and allowing those voices to be heard by policymakers and key decision-makers. The two always go hand-in-hand. Systems change based only on legislation and policy becomes dry and arid without the human heart of grassroots action. Grassroots action alone has the possibility of losing its tremendous potential to change frameworks for all people, even those who are not involved in the movement.

All of this thinking was given greater poignancy when I visited a new Incredible Edible group starting up in Rochdale. The group had previously run food distribution and a pay-as-you-feel café, but was keen to avoid a kind of dependency model. Therefore they decided to create urban growing spaces where people could use their talents to grow fruits and vegetables, harvest them, cook them, and share them together. The conversation about this was happening in the same room which, in 1844, had been the meeting place for a group who became known as the Rochdale Society of Equitable Pioneers. This group of people were troubled by the quality and prices of food that they were able to buy in their local community and similarly decided to club together in order to purchase that food and to share it with each other at fair prices. This group of pioneers became known as the Cooperative Movement. That movement for over a hundred and fifty years ensured fair food prices, fair trade, a just business model, ethical banking, funerals, furniture supply, insurance, and a whole host of other things that made life better. Movements which begin with the focus on achievable small actions for the common good are not different from movements which create long-term systems change, they are part of the same continuum and they grow from the same culture.

Over the next decade, we face rebuilding from a global pandemic, and the needs of our world to live profoundly differently. We do this in order

"NEVER DOUBT THAT A SMALL GROUP OF THOUGHTFUL, COMMITTED CITIZENS CAN CHANGE THE WORLD; INDEED, IT'S THE ONLY THING THAT EVER HAS." MARGARET MEAD

"THESE DIFFERENT ELEMENTS ENABLE US TO LIVE HOPEFULLY TODAY KNOWING THAT WE'VE PLAYED A PART IN BENDING THE ARC OF HISTORY TO ITS BEST DESTINY.

to deliver environmental and social justice. All of these elements, in a changing the world, remain equally important. Each contribution from each group, each individual, matters because it builds together to a better future. A future where we measure human good not by Gross Domestic Product but by a more human and planetary centred set of criteria.

At Incredible Edible we don't have all the answers to these challenges, but we do have a part of the story. We hold together as a movement because we value the unique contribution of each person. We continue to grow our passionate grassroots groups, we campaign for the right to grow, and we advocate for systems change. Hand-in-hand these different elements enable us to live hopefully today knowing that we've played a part in bending the arc of history to its best destiny.

MO BULBROOK

WORKING WITH OTHERS

COVID-19 has deepened existing inequalities, starkly highlighting that the poorest and most vulnerable communities have been hit the hardest. It has put a spotlight on economic inequalities and fragile social safety nets which fail to meet the basic needs of many of our communities including food insecurity, physical and mental health issues, and isolation. At the same time, social, political and economic inequalities have amplified the impacts of the pandemic.

As tragic and destructive as this is, the looming climate and environmental impacts will have greater and more severe consequences – the warning lights are already flashing! We cannot resolve global warming, loss of biodiversity, depletion of non-renewable resources and degradation of our land, oceans and rivers without reducing the widening local and global poverty and inequality. They are all interconnected and now more than ever, we must radically alter the way we live and work and adopt a more ethical economic system.

The Incredible Edible movement is an inclusive, 'if you eat, you're in', kinder, connected communities with emphasis on locally based food growing, sharing learning, and supporting local businesses. With over one hundred and fifty UK groups, and many more internationally, Incredible Edible shows what can be done to harness the power of committed individuals and communities. How can we grow, influence and drive wider changes?

Interconnectedness & interdependence exists from the cellular to the universal. We all know how our diet impacts both short term and long-term physical health and that physical wellbeing has a direct bearing on our emotional wellbeing, and vice versa. This dynamic interconnectedness and interdependence exists in all human created systems and in the natural world. These all overlap with action in one area having an

Board member and director of Incredible Edible CIC.

Mo is an Angel Investor and Non-Exec director and advisor for start-up and early stage enterprises as well as a member of the Ashoka Support Network for social enterprises. A former board director and commercial director of Cheapflights Media and Momondo Group, she specialises in strategic, operational and organizational infrastructure development.

"A KINDER AND MORE INCLUSIVE SOCIETY MEANS THAT EVERYTHING AND EVERYONE MUST CHANGE.

impact, negative or positive, in one or several other systems.

The greatest imbalance we have created as a human species is disconnecting the environment from ourselves, creating the climate change and environmental degradation crisis that is now greatly threatening our future. Our world is a very complex web and layers of interconnected and interdependent, physical-ecological-social-behavioural-economic systems. Now more than ever, it is imperative that we bring this awareness of interconnectedness into our consciousness and inform our behaviour as well as the systems we are part of, work in, set up, or influence. It is key to our well-being as well as that of our planet.

Prominent forces have disturbed the ecosystems in aggressive ways - the Industrial Revolution, the technical revolution, globalisation and capitalism – there is no doubt that they have greatly advanced our society, but this has come at a great cost. Our economic system relies on consumption of goods and services by individuals and drives the engine that creates jobs and wealth.

Overconsumption and drive for cheaper products comes at a huge cost to the environment and devaluation of human labour. Lots of our food in the supermarkets, as well as our clothes and other consumables, are only cheap because of very cheap labour, often in poorer countries with little or no worker protection. Intensive farming, lack of animal welfare, and pollution from production, packaging and transport play their part. There is an argument that food needs to be cheaper for many with low income. This has often led to subsidies that has led to more industrial farming and growing of monocultures leading to greater environmental damage. In addition, subsidies in the developed world come at the expense of poor countries who cannot compete with subsidised products.

This economic model, consumer and profit driven, is just not sustainable. Clearly the economic system needs to change with more robust and stronger regulations of financial markets globally and a move away from GDP growth as a main measure of development.

However, our economic system is intrinsically interconnected to our personal way of living. How we live and work and consume must change too. Conscious awareness of interconnectedness needs to be part of our lives and inform our personal decisions.

Commerce, a significant part of interconnectedness, is also highly innovative and creative. Without it we would not have had the breakthroughs whether in medicine, energy, education, engineering or any other areas. Most companies are also not the "baddies". In fact majority of the people in the UK are either self-employed, about fifteen percent, while around sixty percent of us work in small companies, Many small and large commercial organisations work closely with social enterprises, with charities, and look after their staff, such as Patagonia, Kellogg's, Triodos, UBS, Unilever, M & S, Timpsons, John Lewis, Ikea and Richer Sounds to name just a few. There are also many investment funds which only invest in ethical and social impact enterprises with considerable growth in more recent times.

We clearly require a different approach, not just ourselves as individuals but for a Human and Planetary approach to business. We need a program of economic self-renewal and to work out how we pay for it. For socially inclusive economic growth we need to engage with government, business institutions, community groups and the wider public to influence institutions and policies.

Moreover, a system change that creates a kinder and more inclusive society means that EVERYTHING and EVERYONE must change, and that includes all organisations whether they are community groups, government and non-profit organisations as well as commercial enterprises. This is easier to write, than to implement. Having myself worked in commercial enterprises for many years, as well as a great deal with charities and social enterprises, it is often easier to change the culture of business organisations than those that are in the third sector.

Incredible Edible has shown that it can bolster and help enterprises change. It has shown how

> **SOCIAL ENTERPRISES LIKE INCREDIBLE EDIBLE...DISRUPT THE STATUS-QUO... SHIFTING THE FOCUS BEYOND NUMBERS, TO PEOPLE AND VALUES. [THEY] CAN PROMOTE A PARADIGM SHIFT...AFTER ALL BUSINESSES TOO NEED TO ADAPT IF THEY ARE TO SURVIVE.**

"THE STRENGTH OF INCREDIBLE EDIBLE IS THAT IT LIES BOTH AT THE GRASSROOTS LEVEL WITH INDEPENDENT GROUPS ROOTED IN LOCAL COMMUNITIES AS WELL AS AT THE REGIONAL AND NATIONAL LEVEL AS A COMMUNITY INTEREST COMPANY (CIC).

we can have fairer, healthier and ecologically viable communities with a new way of working and living. Businesses need to be an essential part of the system change. Neither aid/NGOs, government or the market alone can solve the environmental or the poverty & inequality problems.

Social enterprises and grassroots movements have little resources, power or capabilities to reach the tipping point needed for wider change. Commerce can be the engine that drives this. The strength of Incredible Edible is that it lies both at the grassroots level with independent groups rooted in local communities as well as at the regional and national level as a Community Interest Company (cic). Many groups may just want to engage more local citizens, whilst many are already engaged with NHS, schools, local councils, other community groups and local enterprises. A social enterprise, however, may struggle with scaling up, whether it's requiring a small amount of funding for seeds and tools, or to expand its reach and activities. Through co-innovation, joint go-to-market strategies, and partnerships between purpose-driven corporations and social enterprises, both parties can exponentially accelerate their impact.

The foundational economy – local jobs in local communities supporting local spending – can drive regional growth, however in most cases it is stuck in a low skills-low productivity-low wage equilibrium. We need a fundamental rethink of how we train and educate people in such a way that it allows for the ongoing shifting and changing of what has been traditional work. Incredible Edible can be at the forefront and create suitable training to ensure that we provide practical and leadership skills across a range of areas. Creating localised hubs for sharing experience and disseminating innovation and best-practice among organisations, enabling local businesses to adopt and adapt, using stories from peers and access to like-minded people to bounce your ideas off, this is a way forward.

Social enterprises like Incredible Edible, rooted in local communities, bring an agile culture and innovative solutions. They can solve some of the toughest challenges faced by their communities by working directly with those affected. Not only do they present a far more reflective representation of community needs, but they also provide access to a network of key players in the local ecosystem across the value chain. In turn, corporations can bring their own networks, financial resources, brand recognition, and management know-how to propel these enterprises forward.

Of course, when we engage with commercial corporations, we need to ensure they do genuinely act in good faith and not simply for their PR/marketing exercise. Due diligence on their intent is essential. There may also be a need to acknowledge controversial and poor historic records whether in labour management, exploitation, environmental damage or even slavery links. However, this is not simply a problem for commercial enterprises but for many non-profit organisations too. Incredible Edible is about creating positive change, so should we not work with these organisations if they can demonstrate a genuine intent to change?

Incredible Edible, along with other social enterprises, can play a significant part in disrupting the status-quo in the commercial industry and shift the focus beyond numbers to people and values. It can promote a paradigm shift, aligning personal values to work ethics from like-minded businesses, to promote positive social and environmental impact alongside financial returns that are not just growth and profit driven. After all businesses too need to adapt if they are to survive.

"CORPORATIONS CAN BRING THEIR OWN NETWORKS, FINANCIAL RESOURCES, BRAND RECOGNITION, AND MANAGEMENT KNOW-HOW TO PROPEL COMMUNITY ENTERPRISES FORWARD.

LAURIE PEAKE

DIGGING DEEP

"Artists are good at slipping between the institutional walls to expose the layers of emotional and esthetic resonance in our relationships to place".

Lucy Lippard, 2013

"Digging deep is what art is all about."

Agnes Dene, 2019

Forty years ago, Agnes Denes planted a massive wheat field on a landfill site in the shadow of the then Twin Towers on the infertile rubble that was taken from the World Trade Centre as it was built. The sight of acres of amber wheat waving in the breeze in downtown Manhattan, facing the Statue of Liberty, stopped people in their tracks to reflect momentarily, perhaps unconsciously and in passing, on the relationship between global economics, the earth and food.

More than 1,000 pounds of the wheat were harvested, which then travelled to 28 cities around the world in an exhibition called the International Art Show for the end of World Hunger (1987–1990), which provided visitors with seeds to plant. The hay went to Manhattan's mounted police to feed their horses. "The harvest was an incredible feeling. It just made all of us feel so good . . . People from all the office buildings came down to visit us and they prayed for gentle rain, it became their field," In 2019, in an interview with Phoebe Hoban in Architectural Digest, Denes said. "That's exactly what I wanted, the participation and the feeling it created."

Just over 20 years later, in a respectful nod to Denes' grand gesture, Los Angeles environmental artist Lauren Bon planted Not A Cornfield, 32 acres of corn on a brownfield site in downtown Los Angeles left over from the removal of the train yard in the early 20th century, and earmarked to be a historical state park. The site was that of the original pueblo and the once fertile floodplain that had been tended by the Gabrielino and Tongva tribes for millennia before then. It

Board member and director of Incredible Edible CIC.

Laurie Peake specialises in the development of large-scale, long-term art projects in public spaces. She has collaborated with artists in London, Los Angeles, and Liverpool, to co-create work that helps people transform their neighbourhoods, culturally, environmentally, and socially in projects such as Suzanne Lacy's Shapes of Water, Sounds of Hope; Lauren Bon's Bending the River Back into the City; and Jeanne Van Heeswijk's 2Up 2Down.

Laurie is currently Director of Super Slow Way, a cultural development organization and one of Arts Council England's Creative People and Places programmes, located along the Leeds & Liverpool Canal corridor in Pennine Lancashire.

had become the vast terminus of the railway lines constructed across the continent in the late 1800s to build, populate and feed the fast-growing city. The trains brought wheat and corn from the prairies of the Mid-West to supply the city's bottomless appetite, unable to feed itself on a land now dessicated, with its river encased in a concrete jacket.

"The corn itself, a powerful icon for millennia over large parts of Central America and beyond, can serve as a potent metaphor for those of us living in this unique megalopolis. . . ," explained Bon, "By bringing attention to this site throughout the Not A Cornfield process we will also bring forth many questions about the nature of urban public space, about historical parks in a city so young and yet so diverse. About the questions of whose history would a historical park in the city center [sic] actually describe, and about the politics of land use and its incumbent inequities. Indeed, Not A Cornfield is about these very questions, polemics, arguments and discoveries. It is about redemption and hope." The field became a focus for conversations with the diverse communities that lived around it, including Chinese, Latino and indigenous peoples, coming together on a space they began to retake as their own.

Both projects made visible and undeniable the impact that modern humans have on the earth and the distance that they have put between our lives and the land which sustains us. They are grand, radical acts by women who work as artists. In the 19th century they might have been history painters – holding up a mirror to society and asking difficult questions – speaking truth to power. Instead of applying oil to huge canvases or carving into great lumps of marble, they work with the land and the people that live on it or, perhaps more accurately in these urban contexts, alongside it. They are brave, bold figures in the terrain of art that seeks to go beyond the metaphorical representation of society, to create catalysts for its transformation, by carving out new, previously unimagined spaces, with the people that live there and others that have authority over it. Their actions ask 'what if?' and 'why not?'. They ask the big questions that no one else has thought to or dared to or, if so, have not found a powerful way of asking them and

...TO QUOTE AGNES DENE, 'DIGGING DEEP IS WHAT ART IS ALL ABOUT.'

being heard.

These works are actions, not just polemics and metaphors, but active deeds that call into question land-use policy and demonstrate that it could be, to quote architect Teddy Cruz, "a generative tool that organizes activity and economy...[and that] new knowledge exchange corridors can be produced, between the specialized knowledge of institutions and the ethical knowledge of 'community', and artists can have a role to facilitate this exchange, occupying the gap between the visible and the invisible." Above all, they are inspiring, awe-inspiring, and great art should always inspire awe. More importantly, they serve as inspiration on the ground, on the land, in the neighbourhoods they work in, with the people that live there. Although they may achieve significant physical transformation, what they do becomes secondary to why and the challenges they throw down to authority. These works propose an alternate reality in an aesthetic object that looks and feels very different from its surroundings, and creates a space of possibility where new futures can be imagined and crafted.

In the early 2000s, whole neighbourhoods in Liverpool were devastated by the Housing Market Renewal Intitiative. This took the form of mass demolition of 19th century housing stock in a bid to stimulate the construction industry and the housing market in post-industrial towns and cities across the north of England. Dutch artist Jeanne van Heeswijk was invited to a blighted corner of the city called Anfield. Here terraced houses sat in traumatised rows, some half demolished, windows and doors 'tinned up' with steel, in the shadow of the great football ground of the same name. Swathes of bare earth and piles of rubble lay between the homes of families who were trying to survive there; it looked like a war zone but they hadn't been evacuated. Jeanne walked the streets, talking to them – they had a lot to say to anyone who would listen. And she listened.

Over the weeks and months, an ever-growing group of people came to the conclusion they needed a space to meet and talk, beyond the street. The bakery on the corner became that space; for almost a century it had been a haven,

GANDHI'S CONCEPT OF 'KHADI', SIMPLE HOMESPUN FABRIC, REPRESENTED THE BROADER SYMBOLISM OF HIS SWADESHI PHILOSOPHY OF SELF-RELIANCE WHICH WAS DEPENDENT ON PEOPLE'S RIGHT TO LAND.

> ## "WHATEVER WE DO, BE IT FULFILLING THE MOST BASIC NEEDS OF FOOD, CLOTHING AND SHELTER, OR THE LESS TANGIBLE NEEDS OF COMMUNITY AND HOPE, WE ARE ALWAYS TAKEN BACK TO THE LAND.

with warm bread and a caring family of bakers, but it closed, unable to make ends meet with such a reduced and beleaguered customer base. Adopting the motto, 'Loaf by Loaf, Brick by Brick, We Build Ourselves', they did just that. Residents brought what they could; Fred held philosophy discussions on a Tuesday night called 'Pie in the Sky' and Sue would bring in cake. They invited regular guest speakers and the space, tired, dirty and cold, became the site for lively public discussion and planning sessions where people started to think and talk about what the area could and should be. Meetings were always interrupted by passers-by coming in to buy bread, until it became unavoidable that someone needed to learn to bake it. Just as its closure reflected Anfield's decline, so the prospect of re-opening it suggested the possibility of a future, and Homebaked was born. Cleaning, rearranging, painting and baking transformed the tired little shop on the corner into a beacon of hope which housed a Community Land Trust to take on the responsibility for the development of the bakery building and future community assets, notably affordable housing, and, of course, the bakery.

In April 2021, on the outskirts of Blackburn's town centre, a piece of disused land became the unexpected place of an experiment. The land was given over by the council and over 112 days, people from the neighbourhood and beyond planted, grew, nurtured and harvested a half acre of flax. It was then flipped, dried, 'retted', and hand processed into fibre. It was collected by one of the few people in Britain who knew how to spin this into yarn, to dye it using natural indigo dye, also grown in Lancashire, and then weave this thread into linen. This fabric will be made into a pair of dungarees for the youngest volunteer on the flax field who, at 3 years old, is the first 'Homegrown/Homespun' garment made by Community Clothing in the town.

In late September 1931, Mahatma Gandhi came to the UK on his homespun campaign and was invited to Darwen, Lancashire at the invitation of its millworkers to demonstrate their plight due to the Indian boycott of their textiles. In the 90th anniversary year of that visit, the textile industry in Lancashire has all but disappeared but Gandhi's swadeshi philosophy, of homespun self-sufficiency, with a closed loop of local production and use, takes on a renewed relevance in this moment of climate emergency. Gandhi's concept of 'khadi', simple homespun fabric, represented the broader symbolism of his Swadeshi philosophy of self-reliance which was dependent on people's right to land.

Whatever we do, be it fulfilling the most basic needs of food, clothing and shelter, or the less tangible needs of community and hope, we are always taken back to the land. The aims of Incredible Edible, to create lasting physical connections between people and their land, are met in the stories told in this book. They are also met by anyone, from artists to large corporations, who have the vision to recognise this simple truth of connection. Finally, they are met by everyone who wants to play a part in creating a kinder prosperity for themselves, their neighbours and the planet.

THE FIELD BECAME A FOCUS FOR CONVERSATIONS.

PART FIVE

CONTACT & PLANT GLOSSARY

GROUP CONTACT INFORMATION

Incredible Edible groups worldwide can be contacted through www.incredibleedible.org.uk

Abergele and Pensarn
edibleabergeleandpensarn@yahoo.com
facebook.com/edibleabergeleandpensarn

Acassuso
instagram.com/huertavereda

Barnet
ie.barnet@yahoo.co.uk
Facebook: IncredibleEdibleBarnet
Twitter: IncEdibleBarnet

Beeston
incredibleediblebeeston@gmail.com
Facebook: Incredible Edible Beeston
Instagram: incredibleediblebeeston

Camberwell
thorlandsgardens@gmail.com
www.incredibleediblelambeth.org/location/
thorlands-gardens

Cergy Pontoise
noel.constans@lesincroyablescomestibles.fr
www.incroyablescomestibles.fr

Community Gardens Australia
info@communitygarden.org.au

Conwy Town
edibleconwy@gmail.com
facebook.com/Incredible-Edible-Conwy-Bwyd-
Bendigedig-Conwy-154686034717155

Dunstable
incredibleedible395@gmail.com

Garforth
grow@ediblegarforth.org.uk
www.ediblegarforth.org.uk
Facebook,Twitter & Instagram: ediblegarforth

Greystones
helen.mcclelland@greystoneset.ie

Harrogate
WrightS@cvps.rklt.co.uk & CawteD@cvps.rklt.co.uk
www.coppicevalley.com
Facebook: @coppicevalleyprimaryschool
Instagram: coppicevalleyprimary
01423 563760

Inverness
incredibleedibleinverness@gmail.com
@incredibleedibleinverness
07960301753

Lambeth
www.incredibleediblelambeth.org/location/
thorlands-gardens

Leicester
malcolmheaven@btinternet.com

Les Incroyables Comestibles
www.lesincroyablescomestibles.fr

Llandrindod
food@transitionllandrindod.org.uk
www.transitionllandrindod.org.uk

Marshland
Incredibleediblemarshland@gmail.com
facebook.com/Incredible-Edible-
Marshland-562378197619614
07901165349

Munster
www.lesincroyablescomestibles.fr
contact@lesincroyablescomestibles.fr

New Mills
incredible.edible.new.mills@gmail.com
www.ienewmills.wordpress.com/

Norwich
edibleeast@gmail
www.comedibleeast.org.uk

Porthmadog
ediblemadog@gmail.com
facebook.com/ediblemadog

Robertsbridge
info@robertsbridgehelpinghands.co.uk
www.Robertsbridgehelpinghands.co.uk

Rutherglen
eugenie@grow73.org
www.grow73.org
Facebook & Instagram: @Grow73

Salford
facebook.com/groups/422368441235863

San Isidro
instagram.com/huertavereda

South Ormsby
Instagram: ieso_communitygarden
Facebook: IE South Ormsby Community Garden

Southall
info@southalltransition.org
www.southalltransition.org

PLANT GLOSSARY

Achocha - *cyclanthera pedata*
Amaranth - *amaranthus spp*

Basil - *ocimum basilicum*
Bay laurel - *laurus nobilis*
Beetroot - *beta vulgaris*
Blackcurrant - *ribes nigrum*
Broad bean - *vicia faba*
Broccoli - *brassica oleracea var. italica*

Chickpeas - *cicer arietinum*
Chilli peppers - *capsicum annuum 'Cayenne'*
Coriander - *coriandrum sativum*
Courgettes - *cucurbita pepo*
Cabbage - *brassica oleracea var. capitata*
Cavolo Nero (Kale) - *brassica oleracea var. palmifolia*
Cherry tomato - *solanum lycopersicum var. cerasiforme*
Chervil - *anthriscus cerefolium*
Chives - *allium schoenoprasum*
Cornflowers - *centaurea cyanus*

Dandelion - *taraxacum officinale*
Dudi aka Calabash - *lagenaria siceraria*

Fennel - *foeniculum vulgare*
French bean - *phaseolus vulgaris*

Garlic - *allium sativum*
Garlic Chives - *allium tuberosum*
Globe Artichokes - *cynara cardunculus var. scolymus*
Good King Henry - *blitum bonus-henricus*
Gooseberry - *ribes uva-crispa*

Hops - *humulus lupulus*

Lavender - *lavandula spica*
Lettuce - *lactuca sativa*

Marigold - *calendula arvensis*
Mint – *mentha spp*
Mizuna aka Water greens - *brassica rapa var. niposinica*

Mustard greens - *brassica juncea*
Nasturtium - *tropaeolum majus*

Onion - *allium cepa*

Pak choi - *brassica rapa ssp. chinensis*
Parsley - *petroselinum crispum*
Peach tree - *prunus persica*
Peas - *pisum sativum*
Pepper - *capsicum annuum*
Peppermint - *mentha × piperita*
Purple sage - *salvia officinalis 'purpurascens'*
Purple sprouting broccoli - *brassica oleracea italica*

Radish - *raphanus sativus*
Raspberry - *rubus idaeus*
Redcurrant - *ribes rubrum*
Red Peppers - *capsicum annuum 'bell'*
Rhubarb - *rheum × hybridum*
Ribwort Plantain - *plantago lanceolata*
Rosemary - *salvia rosmarinus*

Sage - *salvia officinalis*
Sharks' fin melon aka Figleaf gourd - *cucurbita ficifolia*
Spinach - *spinacia oleracea*
Strawberries - *fragaria ananassa*
Sunflowers - *helianthus*
Swiss chard - *beta vulgaris var, cicla*

Thyme - *thymus vulgaris*
Tomatoes - *solanum lycopersicum*

Welsh Onion - *allium fistulosum*
Wild Violet - *viola odorata*